The Globetrotter's Guide

Essential Skills for Budget Travel

The Globetrotter's Guide

Essential Skills for Budget Travel

Guide

Wayne Smits
Caryl E. Dolinko

Red Deer College Press

The Publishers
Red Deer College Press
56 Avenue & 32 Street Box 5005
Red Deer Alberta Canada T4N 5H5

Acknowledgments
Cover and text design by Boldface Technologies.
Printed and bound in Canada by Webcom for Red Deer College
Press.
The authors gratefully acknowledge the kind assistance of Dr.
Donna Spaner for her generous guidance through the medical
information and Dr. Lisa Barnes for her knowledge of women's
health issues; Heather Markham and Anita Jenkins for their
advice and participation in the initial publication of this guide.

Financial support provided by the Alberta Foundation for the
Arts, a beneficiary of the Lottery Fund of the Government of
Alberta, and by the Canada Council, the Department of Cana-
dian Heritage and Red Deer College.

COMMITTED TO THE DEVELOPMENT OF CULTURE AND THE ARTS

THE CANADA COUNCIL | LE CONSEIL DES ARTS
FOR THE ARTS | DU CANADA
SINCE 1957 | DEPUIS 1957

5 4 3 2

Canadian Cataloguing in Publication Data

Smits, Wayne, 1959–
The globetrotter's guide
Previous ed. has title: The complete guide to independent travel
ISBN 0-88995-172-1
1. Travel. I. Dolinko, Caryl E. (Caryl Eve), 1963– II. Title.
III. Title: The complete guide to independent travel.
G151.S65 1998   910'.2'02   C98-910094-4

To all those whose love and support
have gotten us this far,
and to the many who made this book possible.
–*Wayne and Caryl*

Contents

Contents

Contents

Preface

Wayne Smits Late one night many years ago, at a send-off party for my first trip abroad, a close friend backed me into a quiet corner and asked, "What is it you hope to find out there?" A pretty deep question for that time of evening, one that caught me a little off guard and brought to mind the saying that travel is "the unrest men miscall delight!" The answer I gave was different than the answer I would give today. And I expect today's answer would be different than tomorrow's. The question itself, however, remains constant over all these years. What is it I really hope to find?

Back then, perhaps travel provided a temporary escape from the banality of early adulthood. It was a time of life when thoughts typically turn to higher education, career and the inevitable cultural insistence of family commitments and responsibilities. But on the other hand, I was genuinely caught up in the excitement, independence and wonder of it all. Travel was an opportunity to journey not just over distance but through time and space, reeling me, from my cultural perspective, hundreds if not thousands of years into the past at the simple expense of a fourteen-hour plane fare. Travel was a real-life historical drama where the stage was always set and the improvised script unfolded moment by moment. There always seemed to be unlimited possibility for tragedy and comedy, danger and romance, suspense and relief, and all the other elements that make good theater great.

And well beyond the immediate and obvious by-products of a travel-stimulated imagination was the realization that life was what you made of it. Anything and everything seemed possible. And it was through this raw reality, for better or worse, that a clearer sense of life emerged and allowed me to be outside my experience looking in. Beyond the horizon lay a part of myself that could never be discovered at home.

In retrospect I had to wonder if I was ever really *looking* for anything. Anything of lasting value, that is. The act of looking seemed to imply conscious effort, and after surviving seven months of Southeast Asia and India on four dollars a day, I returned home skinny and ragged but never feeling stronger and more alive in all my eighteen years. It was a strength that came not from looking and finding, but from throwing myself out there with no safety net and dealing with whatever came my way. For better or worse, this was life, this was independence, this was just like being in a movie! I was young and a hopeless romantic. But after that first trip with all its highs and lows, I could never look at life the same way again. I was smitten with the proverbial (and perennial) travel bug.

And now, many years later as I work on this guide, the question arises once again. What is it that travel offers? What is just over the horizon? What is it that I know can never be found at home? If I could answer those questions with one word, it would be *experience*. But as the expression goes, "Experience comes from bad judgment. Good judgment comes from experience." If we are to savor all that travel has to offer, we must each pay our dues. But how much and for how long is directly related to our ability to adapt to the routine and pitfalls of life on the road. In financial terms this applies to inexperienced travelers who manage to spend half their funds in a quarter of their budgeted time. During this period they learn the do's and don'ts of where, when and how to spend time and money. Once bad judgments are made and lessons are learned, it's not that difficult to stretch the remaining half of the money over the final three quarters of the trip.

But more than money is at stake during this crucial period of adjustment. This is a period of vulnerability when failure may break the whole adventure, and on many occasions there is no going back to undo a moment of careless naïveté. *The Globetrotter's Guide* was written to offer you the good judgment my coauthor and I have derived from travel experience, plus that of the many thousands we have encountered, for life on the road makes storytellers of us all. We cannot and do not wish to rob you of all the mistakes you may make along the way, for these will make you better travelers. But we do hope to hasten the transition from novice to roadwise in the least amount of time and at the least expense.

Although our goal is to make you a better traveler faster, remember that any trip taken is yours and yours alone. There are as many ways of traveling as there are travelers. What you find and how you deal with it will be a reflection of who you are. We all carry personal baggage crammed with our strengths, weaknesses, needs, fears and expectations. Before you leave and along the way, people will suggest how to pack that bag, real or emotional, but you will have final say over what goes where and why. Just try to leave a little space for all that you will inevitably acquire along the way. Whether you are looking for it or not! Bon voyage!

Caryl E. Dolinko When I first started to travel at the age of eighteen, I had great fortune on my side. After the emotional good-byes from my family at the airport, I was drained and slowly becoming apprehensive. What was I doing, going off to the other side of the world on my own?

After I found a seat in the boarding lounge, a nice-looking blond-haired blue-eyed guy sat beside me. Our eyes met, and he smiled sweetly as if he understood how I felt. And as it turned out, he did. On this first day, I was fortunate to have found an experienced globetrotter willing to share the "how to" of overland travel. We struck up a conversation, and I found that he knew my sister. Our ultimate destinations were different, but we would still be spending the nine-hour flight together. He was a few years older and had traveled a great deal, so of course the conversation gravitated in that direction. During the time we spent together, he filled me in on the strategies of traveling with street smarts and insight. I'll never forget him and the essential travel advice he shared with me on that day.

We parted company in Amsterdam, and I didn't see him again for many years. By then I had been to over forty countries on my own, and we were able to share the incredible and common stories that had become so natural to both of us. At the time this is written, I have journeyed on my own to over sixty countries in fourteen years, managing to return home healthy and a lot wiser every time. Travel opened my eyes to a reality many people cannot imagine and gave me a clearer understanding of the meaning of freedom.

When approached to help write this guide, I thought it would be a great opportunity to share the lessons I had learned. If there had been a guidebook like this when I started traveling, I would not have felt so apprehensive so long ago.

Coincidentally, here I sit beside Wayne, that same person I met in the boarding lounge years ago, writing this guide. I hope that with the insight provided in this book, you will begin your journey feeling a little less alone and that you depart armed with enough basic knowledge to get you off the plane and traveling with a healthy sense of confidence, awareness and respect for all the people and experiences you are about to encounter.

Planning

WHY INDEPENDENT OVERLAND TRAVEL?

Passing time in a railway car about to leave the station, Marlene, sitting across from me, was excited but still just a little apprehensive. Three days in Southeast Asia, and she was none the worse for wear, considering the long flight over and the time difference. Second-class sleeper, air-conditioned. Yeah, she'll be all right, I thought, looking forward to a much needed half-night's sleep.

As we talked, her eyes darted to the window. Then came a muffled cry of terror. "Kill it! Kill it!" she screamed, pointing at a small roach scurrying across the armrest. Mildly amused and hoping her reaction was merely an exaggeration, I complied and dispatched the tiny roach with my sandal. When I sat back and the train began to move, she told me that she was indeed terrified of insects. Then she noticed my eyes wander to the wall behind her head, and afraid to turn around, she asked what was wrong. The wall five inches behind her head danced with the movement of at least ten of the same roaches, but bigger. "Nothing," I lied, realizing that her comfort zone was soon to be dramatically altered or it was going to be a long night.

Welcome to the world of budget overland travel.

Independent overland travel is about meeting people and doing incredible things while coping with the excitement, strain, boredom, exhilaration and frustration of being on your own so far from home. It's about endurance, tolerance and the ability to think on your feet. It's keeping your cool when you have every right to lose it completely. It's wondering why in the world you would ever expose yourself to such ridiculous (or amusing) situations and then wondering how you could ever rob yourself of the opportunity not to.

Independent overland travel is about independence and movement. It's not about guided tours, tightly planned itineraries and five-star hotels. It *is* about finding your way from the airport to the hotel, changing money, locating affordable restaurants with palatable food, seeing the sights and protecting your valuables. It's standing in line to buy a bus ticket with your bowels in a knot and then sitting on a cliff (because your bus has stalled out) overlooking a valley of rice paddies, watching the tropical sun set, never feeling more at peace in all your life. It's wiring home for money and then spending the next two weeks broke while attempting to track it down! It's about getting lost and being found, winning and losing, and making it home, happy to have done it once, or ready to rest up, wash your clothes and scrape together enough money to start traveling all over again.

True overland budget travel may not be glamorous, but it's the closest possible experience to everyday life in a foreign country. And for that reason, it's one of the most rewarding ways to go. It will require you to push the boundaries of your comfort zones and do things you would never expect to do in a million years. Not because you may *want* to do them but because if you don't, nobody else will. And when it's done you may sit back and marvel at what you have accomplished, having seen and experienced so much on so little.

WHERE?

Every good trip starts with a good plan. Every good plan starts with an examination of your motives. What are you looking for? Adventure? Exploration? Relaxation? Great suntanning? Good times? Good surf? Or just a chance to get away? The choice is yours. Whatever your goal, budget travel anywhere in the world starts with the knowledge that life is not coming to a theater near you. Knowing what you want will help you decide your destination.

Growing up on the Canadian prairies, where winter temperatures are often cold enough to freeze exposed skin in under a minute, I was determined that my first extended trip abroad would include palm trees, warm weather and tropical beaches. After a few trips, however, I noticed that a country's culture and history were more important. Though I still enjoy a good tropical setting, the diversity of foreign cultures and my excitement at discovering them are what keep overland travel meaningful to me. — WAYNE

WITH WHOM?

Whether you travel by yourself, with a lover, with another couple or with a group of friends, you eventually discover that each has advantages and disadvantages. Your destination and reason for going should help determine whether you wish to travel with a companion or on your own. Traveling on a short trip to an affordable sunspot with a group of friends is fine if you want to party, sow some wild

17

oats or attempt some controversial rites of passage, but it is unrealistic for lengthy overland travel. Two couples traveling together may find harmony for a short period, but lifestyle issues and personal expectations may surface along the way, creating ill feelings that could eventually lead to separate travel plans. Only three options are worth discussing for extended travel: traveling with a friend, traveling with an intimate partner and traveling alone.

With a Friend

Traveling with a friend is one of the best ways to go. With one other person, it's easier to save money by sharing the cost of food, lodging and transportation. Also important is the added security of having someone to watch your valuables while you scout out information, tickets, rooms and anything else that is difficult to do while carrying your belongings. Above all else, traveling with another person allows you to experience things together, share feelings and ideas, and exchange cultural observations. There is the added comfort of knowing somebody is there for you if needed.

But with a partnership comes responsibility and tolerance for differences. Spending many months together on the road, under intense highs and lows, tends to bring out the best and worst in people. Though you might know each other well before leaving, it is likely that you'll discover aspects of each other's character that would not surface under everyday circumstances. You might find that a compatible companion at home is not compatible on the road, so be prepared to compromise.

It helps to be fairly comfortable with the person you hope to travel with because surprises on the road can be inconvenient and costly. For better or worse, you will either return home with a closer friendship than before or find that you are worlds apart.

People who wish to travel with a partner but have nobody available at the time can place ads in university papers or at local meeting places of like-minded people. Health food stores, outdoor shops, travel agencies and youth hostels are just a few places to start your search. This strategy may not *guarantee* a suitable travel partner, but even if you only travel together for a short while, you'll see how easy it is to meet other people. If things don't work, this arrangement makes it easier to separate along the way without too many hard feelings or inconveniences.

If you can't find a suitable travel partner, don't worry and don't postpone your trip. There are so many people traveling these days that you'll find someone compatible heading your way.

With an Intimate Partner

Traveling with an intimate partner can add a strong emotional dimension to any trip, but the one major drawback is the likelihood of being a bit reclusive, whether you are conscious of it or not. When you are with a close partner, your need to approach locals or other travelers is greatly reduced and could prove socially restrictive. Locals also may be a little less likely to approach a foreign couple as opposed to a single traveler.

On Your Own

It is better to travel alone than with a bad companion.
– SENEGALESE PROVERB

In our opinion, traveling on your own is the most flexible and rewarding way to go. When you are by yourself, you move at your own discretion, live on your own budget and cater to your own interests. And unless you are a certified loner, there is unlimited opportunity to practice your social skills. There is no better treatment for introverts than traveling on their own. Personal contact with the local culture will also increase when traveling solo because a single traveler may appear more approachable. It's also much easier for a local to offer a ride, extend an invitation for dinner or let someone stay the night when there is only one person to accommodate.

There may be lonely times in sparsely traveled out-of-the-way locations, but for the most part, wherever you go, there is a very good chance that a lot of people are also heading that way. Others on the road are usually quick to ask about good hotels, share travel tales, split taxi fares, go to dinner or just offer their company. You may, for instance, be sitting by yourself in a restaurant at a table set for two, and locals or other travelers may see the empty seat as an open invitation. You may be on your own, but you are rarely left that way unless you want to be.

Solo travel has the added benefit of forcing you to trust your instincts and not rely on others. The feelings of accomplishment and increased self-esteem that result cannot be measured or imagined. So if you have any inclinations to travel in this fashion, take a chance! You will not be disappointed.

How Much?

Travel, especially in developing countries, can be economical, but how economical is up to you. You must make a budget that takes account of the following: where you are going and for how long, how you wish to travel, what you wish to purchase and what you want to see.

Destination and Length of Stay

Where you are going and how long you expect to stay are the two biggest considerations in establishing a travel budget. It is generally accepted that the average per-day budget is much lower on an extended trip than on a shorter one. The principle reason is that it takes time and experience to learn how to live economically.

The economy of the country or countries through which you choose to travel will also greatly influence your per-day living costs. For this obvious reason, developing countries generally provide the best bang for your buck. In the third world you should be able to sustain yourself on a budget of US$10–20 per day once you've established a routine. In developed regions—such as Europe, Japan, Australia and New Zealand—naturally you will pay more and you will have to adjust your budget accordingly. Depending on the type of lodging, rest and transport you take, costs can run as high as US$50–75 per day. Wherever you go, cutting down on high costs takes just a little extra care and imagination. You can, for example, eat in local diners, take local transport or visit museums and galleries during the off season.

When traveling in Paris, I quickly realized that my per-day budget didn't reflect the high prices charged in restaurants. To counter the problem, I purchased baguettes, cheese, vegetables and wine at the market, and picnicked on park benches with beautiful views of the city. – CARYL

Economy versus Luxury Travel

You generally get (or hope to get) what you pay for, and though you will eventually adjust your standards concerning what is dirty, comfortable and worth it in the long run, we all have our limits of flexibility and tolerance. If you

21

need rooms with attached baths and hot water, western food and air-conditioned transportation, you should expect to pay for them. On the other hand, bathing in the river, eating only steamed rice and always traveling third class will save you money, but these options are not without some psychological or emotional costs.

Between the two extremes is a happy medium. Although it's nice to rent a motorcycle or enjoy a night out on the town, if you do either on a regular basis you should expect to spend a lot more money or stay a lot less time. Ideally, you should develop an ability to rough it in situations that offer few luxuries or facilities. This increases the opportunities for experiencing life off the beaten track. If early signs of travel burnout result, move on to a larger center with more luxuries and give yourself a break. One night of fine dining can change your point of view without breaking the bank. You may be traveling on a shoestring, but try to budget for some luxuries along the way.

> *While traveling in Israel, I craved some homestyle luxuries. In Tel Aviv, I booked a room at the Sheraton and splurged. Room service, videos, queen-sized beds and laundry made me feel wonderfully spoiled and ready to face life on the road again.* –CARYL

Souvenirs and Presents

Of course, you're going to buy something, aren't you? Better include that in your budget. Over the years we have purchased many exotic items, sometimes knowing full well they would be a hassle to carry, wrap, pack or send home, but we bought them nonetheless and have rarely been disappointed. The rugs wear well, the wall hangings look fabulous and the carvings, pottery and knickknacks are all wonderful reminders of times away. The key is to start with a firm budget that you won't change unless that once-in-a-lifetime souvenir comes your way.

Sight-Seeing

Often you can keep your sight-seeing expenses down by tagging along with (or at least within earshot of) a tour group. Their guides are usually well versed in information about the sites and may have tidbits that your guidebook doesn't provide. Unfortunately, this is not always possible, so the more sites you see, the more it will eventually cost. Budget accordingly. Admission to many local attractions like museums is next to nothing. But some cultural events and historic sites are geared toward the upmarket tourist and can be expensive. The best approach is to learn as much as you can about sight-seeing costs before leaving home and make sure you've budgeted enough to see what you want to see.

Anatomy of a Traveler

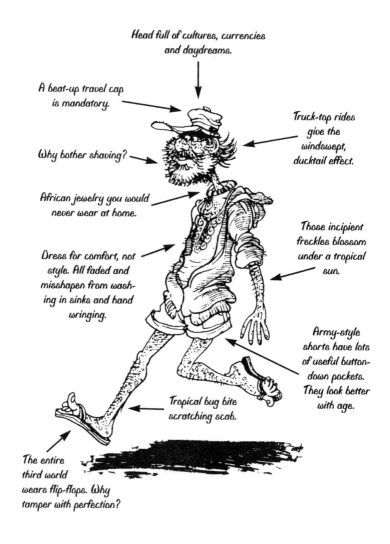

Head full of cultures, currencies and daydreams.

A beat-up travel cap is mandatory.

Truck-top rides give the windswept, ducktail effect.

Why bother shaving?

African jewelry you would never wear at home.

Those incipient freckles blossom under a tropical sun.

Dress for comfort, not style. All faded and misshapen from washing in sinks and hand wringing.

Army-style shorts have lots of useful button-down pockets. They look better with age.

Tropical bug bite scratching scab.

The entire third world wears flip-flops. Why tamper with perfection?

Preparations

In preparing for your trip abroad, try not to let everything pile up until the last minute. It may seem like forever until you leave, but time has an uncanny way of slipping by. Your last few days at home should be reserved for relaxing, socializing and final details that cannot be accomplished sooner. If you procrastinate, you can easily find yourself running around frantically the day before you leave, trying to decide what is a priority and what will ultimately be left undone.

TRAVEL AGENTS

A good travel agent is difficult to find, so shop around. Look for an agent who is able to cater to the kind of travel you hope to do, and who has the practical experience to give advice and suggest options. The agent should be able to provide you with general and current travel information that may be difficult to obtain on your own, such as the political or economic stability of your destination. Your agent also should have the resources to obtain the best possible price on air tickets or alternate routes with the fewest number of hassles and restrictions.

Your travel agent also should have access to lower and midrange accommodation—if you choose to book in advance—and up-to-date transport information. The agent should be able to book and issue your ticket, secure necessary visas, provide insurance and treat you like a valued customer, before, during and even after your trip. Not many travel agencies can accommodate all of the above, but this is at least a helpful list upon which to base your search.

TIPS FOR TRIPS

- If you want the security of booking well in advance, keep in mind that flying on certain days can reduce fares considerably.

- Make sure you are ticketed on a stable airline that will not declare bankruptcy shortly after you've paid. Paying with a credit card might provide bankruptcy protection, but check with your bank first.

- If your agent is having difficulty getting a good price or seating availability on the day you wish to travel, try calling around yourself. Many times you may be able to find what your travel agent can't. Don't be afraid to get on the phone and the internet.

- Discount locations such as Amsterdam, London, Athens and Bangkok are only a few of the places to get airfares from bucket ticket shops for far less than you could by booking and paying for them at home. If you are heading to Africa, for example, instead of buying your full ticket at home, consider buying one to Amsterdam only. From there you will find a cheaper fare to get you the rest of the way. But do not expect to get any help or cooperation from your local travel agent.

- Local holidays tend to disrupt plans for many reasons ranging from hotel vacancies to onward travel arrangements. Keep them in mind when deciding on arrival and departure dates.

- Always leave enough time between connecting flights to account for unexpected delays or early departures.

- Try to secure your airline seating arrangement at the time of booking. If a desired location is unavailable, try calling the airlines after midnight, when cancellations create new options. If there are a few unoccupied seats next to your seat, you may request that the agent block them so you have more room to yourself on long flights.

- If you telephone an airline with a change of plans and you are asked to pay a penalty on your credit card, say you will pay it at the airport instead. Chances are good you will not be charged when checking in.

- When booking your ticket, preorder special meals, consider which side of the plane to sit on (for best scenery) and deal with any other preflight requests you may have.

- Be aware of all conditions and restrictions placed upon your ticket. These may state that it's nonreroutable, nonendorsable, nonrefundable, that it must be used within thirty days of purchase, that it must be used within one year of booking your outbound flight or that a fee may be charged for changes. Any questions you may have about conditions or restrictions should be discussed with your travel agent or the airlines. The back of your ticket will also list restrictions such as allowable baggage weight, illegal firearms, and rules, regulations and laws by which the airline must abide.

- A Miscellaneous Charges Order (MCO) is a coupon issued by airlines for advance payment of an unspecified flight at a future date or instead of a cash refund. MCOs are good for countries that require you to have an onward ticket before granting you permission to enter. If you are traveling overland, you do not want to have to buy a plane ticket for every country with this kind of policy, so in many cases, an MCO will satisfy their conditions.

- Keep in mind that travel agents are not insurance agents. Know what you need and read your insurance policy carefully. You are ultimately responsible for being aware of all the conditions and restrictions. Many policies have limited coverage when dealing with adventure activities like trekking, diving or rafting. If partaking in such activities, it is wise to ensure beforehand that your policy covers medical airlift evacuation in the event you need to be moved for medical reasons from one location to another or to your home country for treatment. If you have questions, bypass your travel agent and talk directly to your insurance company.

- Many times your home insurance policy will cover the loss or theft of personal property while traveling. Check with your insurance agent before leaving.

- It's a good idea to take out insurance for a little longer than you intend to use it provided you have a policy that allows you a refund for any unused portion.

There is always the possibility that you will be held up for one reason or another and may not return home by the time the policy expires.

▱ Record all model and serial numbers of electronic equipment you'll be taking along and insure them for replacement value, not what you paid for them.

I remember times when friends dropping me off at the airport eagerly drew straws to see who was going to be the lucky one to pay for, and thus become the beneficiary of, my accident insurance! – WAYNE

Eurail Passes

A Eurail Pass lets you travel on Europe's 100,000-mile (160,900-km) railway network through seventeen countries. Passes must be purchased before arriving in Europe and are for first and second class travel with a variety of itinerary options, which include the Eurail Youth Flexipass, Eurail Youth Pass, Eurail Saver Pass and the Eurail Flexipass. Each comes with its advantages and is designed to accomodate different itineraries. Your travel agent can provide you with the most current information and prices.

DOCUMENTS AND MONEY

Once you have decided on your destination and length of stay, who you will be traveling with and how much your trip will cost, your next step is obtaining the proper documentation. These include passport and visas; traveler's checks, cash and credit cards; vaccination cards and medical documents; and personal identification.

Passports

Technically, a passport is a document issued by your government identifying you as a citizen in good standing. It also requests permission from a foreign government to let you freely enter and pass through their country while offering lawful aid and protection. But in reality a passport is little more than a practical method for internal security and immigration to keep track of the comings and goings of all foreigners. It also will be needed for bank transactions, hotel registrations, bureaucratic requests and purchases such as permits, travel passes and so on. A passport is not a problem to obtain, but the sooner you apply the better because it may take some time to process. If you already have a passport, check to make sure it is valid and will remain valid during the entirety of your trip.

TIPS FOR TRIPS

◪ It's a good idea to photocopy the cover and the photo and identification pages of your passport. Place the copies back to back and laminate them. This facsimile will prove useful in many situations not requiring the use of your real passport.

I was traveling in Nigeria just eight days after the country had opened its doors to tourists. As a friend and I drove along the highways, we were frequently delayed at military road checks by soldiers. I didn't feel comfortable opening my money belt to find my real passport, so I showed my laminated, photocopied passport and it was never refused, questioned or scrutinized. – CARYL

◪ All passports issued by the same country look alike, and these may resemble passports from other countries. So it's a good idea to distinguish yours from the rest at borders and embassies. Try stretching a rubberband down the spine or drawing a stripe down the paper edge with a marker.

◪ Once you have obtained your passport, memorize the number, date and place of issue, and expiration date. Knowing this will cut down on the amount of time it usually takes to fill out arrival cards, hotel registrations and so forth.

◾ If you'll be doing a lot of traveling over the next few years, you will accumulate a large number of visas, stamps, permits and declarations. You may want to look into a commercial passport, which gives you more than the average number of pages and saves you the trouble of reapplying for a new passport when your regular one is filled.

◾ If you do not have a commercial passport and run out of pages while traveling, you may be able to apply for extension pages at your embassy abroad.

◾ Make sure you receive a receipt if you leave your passport with any foreign consulate. The receipt should contain all necessary identification information and a date when you are to pick it up.

Personal Identification

Most travelers consider a passport the only piece of personal identification, but it's only a beginning. Most countries you travel through are bureaucratically obsessed with the need to know exactly who you are and where you come from, so it's important carry personal identification, whether it's your passport, a driver's license or a birth certificate. Apart from your official travel documents there are others that you may want to consider getting before leaving home or while on the road.

Tips for Trips

◾ If you are a student, contact your registrar's office to apply for a student card that provides discounts on travel and accommodation. If you have applied to an institution but are not yet enrolled, you will need to get a letter signed by a dean of admission on school stationery stating that you are enrolled in that particular educational institution. With this letter you can apply for a card at a school office somewhere overseas. If you do not have access to a letter of admission and would still like a card, then you will have to wait until reaching a city like Bangkok, where bootleg student cards are available but are of dubious merit.

◾ A Federation of Youth Travel Organization (FYTO) membership card is very much like a student card, but its value is limited. You do not need to be actively enrolled in school, but you must be under twenty-five years of age. FYTO membership cards can be obtained from university travel shops or accredited post-secondary institutions.

▱ If you plan to stay at a youth hostel run by Hosteling International, a youth hostel card is a must.

▱ If you are planning to rent, buy or operate a motor vehicle while away, you will need an international driver's license. An auto club membership may also prove useful and can be purchased for a nominal fee by presenting passport-sized photographs and your current driver's license at your automobile association.

▱ If you plan to find work, do not bring resumes and letters of reference with you. Have them faxed or couried to you once you reach your destination.

▱ If you are leaving the country with expensive or sophisticated electronic equipment, you may want to have receipts proving you bought them in your home country, or register them with customs and have them documented. If you don't have receipts when returning home, you may have difficulty if customs officers become suspicious. In some countries, expect to have any expensive or hard-to-obtain equipment documented in your travel papers. You may even be asked to pay a deposit to ensure that you leave with everything you brought in.

Visas

Unlike passports, visas can be a dicey affair to obtain. It would seem logical to obtain as many visas as possible in your home country in order to save time and trouble during your travels. However, this is not always advisable or practical. Many times it takes longer and is more costly to get the visas at home than abroad. Also, depending on which countries you plan to visit, there is no guarantee that they are represented by an embassy or consulate in your home country. Additional problems are the bureaucracy and restrictions on the validation of a visa. It may be many months before you show up at the frontier of a particular country, and your visa may have expired by then. There is also the possibility that you may change your itinerary. The

best thing to do is to collect necessary visas as you go. If you need a visa for the country you will be landing in, always obtain it from the country you're currently in. Check with your travel agent, current guidebooks, airlines or an appropriate consular office.

In the past, traveling on a Canadian passport saved me a lot of time and hassle because many countries did not require a visa before entering. In 1982 I was with an American woman whom I had met in Israel. We were checking in at the airport in Athens for a flight to Bombay when the ticket agent asked my companion for her visa. Embarrassed, she looked at me with the realization that she hadn't even thought of it. We were disheartened at the thought of spending several more days in Greece while awaiting her visa and were relieved when the airline official said, "Don't worry. It's India. Just show up. You'll work it out." Cracking a conspiratorial smile, she gave us our boarding passes and we were on our way. Ten hours and $10 "baksheesh" (a tip or bribe) later, we made an easy entry into India. – WAYNE

TIPS FOR TRIPS

- When filling in a visa application, your reason for traveling should be tourism. Anything else could cause lengthy discussion and unwanted questioning. The most problematic professions to declare are journalist, writer, photograher or military personnel on vacation.

- If you are applying for a visa where you may not intend to stay long, or if the time to process it is longer than anticipated, ask if you can apply for your visa at that location but pick it up at another.

- If you are returning to the same country on a number of occasions, apply for a multiple entry visa.

- Be aware of problems that can arise when you attempt to enter a country with a visa stamped by a country that is viewed as unfriendly or antagonistic. For example, trying to enter an Arab country with a used visa from Israel can be tricky. In this situation, request that your visa and all accompanying stamps be put on a separate piece of paper so they do not show up in your passport.

- At times, a border or consular official will demand that you have more than sufficient funds for your stay in the country. If it looks like you will not have enough money by their estimates for the time that you plan to stay, then accept whatever time you are allotted and apply for an extension later, armed with borrowed traveler's checks or a credit card.

- It might be helpful to backdate your visa application in embassies that are known for long processing times. Sometimes they process them simply by the date that the application was submitted.

- If asked how long you plan to be in the country, always request the maximum amount of time.

- If asked for an itinerary, be vague and find out if you are going to be held to it.

- If you must apply for a visa to a country in turmoil, it may be better to obtain it in your own country before leaving.

- If you expect problems with your visa or are short of funds, you are more likely to find an official open to negotiation at a land border crossing than at an international airport.

After a long flight from London, I arrived exhausted in South Africa. I waited my turn in the immigration line. After finally making it to the officer I realized my problems had just begun when he asked, "Where is your visa?" I didn't quite know what he was talking about. I had a passport, I had money, I had an onward flight, but I had forgotten to check if a visa was needed. Big mistake!

I was told that I couldn't come into the country and that I would have to return on the next flight to London. I was devastated. I had finally arrived on the African continent and was now being told to leave. I made a few phone calls, talked to a few people and with the assistance of a gentleman at the Canadian Embassy, I was granted a transit visa good for one week. I left the airport feeling like an idiot for not having done the most essential part of my travel homework. Since that time, I have never ventured out my front door without wondering if I should first inquire about the required visas. – CARYL

Traveler's Checks, Cash and Credit Cards

In the immortal words of Miss Piggy (the Muppet), "Less is not more; more is more!"

When it comes to money and travel, you should always try to have a little more than you think you should have and access to a lot more than you think you will need. But whatever the sum you're planning to carry, the bulk should be in the form of traveler's checks, leaving the remainder in cash.

Traveler's checks are by far the most secure form of travel currency, offering you refund peace of mind in the unfortunate circumstance that they are lost or stolen. (No, this is not an advertisement!) In choosing a company, go with a name that is reputable, well recognized and accepted worldwide. Next, consider the company's ability to provide a quick refund in an emergency or, if that is not possible, what they are prepared to do to hold you over.

To the banks and money changers of the world, local demand dictates whether traveler's checks command a more favorable rate of return than cash when exchanging currency. The major difference between the two is that only cash is negotiable on the black market.

When deciding what form of currency to carry, remember that the American dollar is in the highest demand and is the most widely traded. Any other stable currency is an option, including English pounds, German marks, Japanese yen and French or Swiss francs. Lesser currencies like the Canadian or Australian dollar are passable in large cities or popular tourist spots, but in general the American dollar is strongly recommended.

TIPS FOR TRIPS

- Try to carry your traveler's checks or cash in large denominations such as hundreds with a few hundred in fifties and twenties, which are useful when you do not require much local currency. A good reason for larger denominations is that many exchange houses or banks will charge you a commission or tax on the number of checks or bills exchanged, so it would cost much more to cash five twenties than a single hundred. If you need smaller denominations you can always exchange your larger checks for smaller ones along the way.

- Make a list of all your traveler's check serial numbers and cross them off as you use them, remembering to keep a record of the date and place. Keep this record separate from all other travel documents.

- Keep your original traveler's check purchase receipt with bank name and location and leave a photocopy at home in your home file (more on this later).

- Re-count and examine your traveler's checks when they are out of your possession for any length of time. A thief may have stolen a few from the middle, hoping you would not notice the crime for some time.

Travel with a few hundred dollars in cash in varying denominations. Cash commands a higher rate of exchange in countries with a black market and allows quick transactions when local currency is not available because banks may be closed or too difficult to get to. If you get caught up in a bribe situation, having cash to work with encourages quick negotiations. Fifty dollars' worth of ones and fives are convenient for small transactions like cab fares and tips. Larger bills like fifties and hundreds will bring a higher rate of return in some banks and on the black market.

Also try to carry a hundred-dollar bill hidden somewhere safe (sewn into your belt, for example). This stash can be called upon if you ever have the misfortune of being separated from your funds. You can always get your traveler's checks replaced, but what if you are hundreds of miles from any refund facility during a holiday or a transport strike? A cold hard stash of cash will be a lifesaver.

In the early days of overland travel, credit cards were not readily recognized or accepted in the major cities, let alone off the beaten path. Times have changed though, and credit cards are now accepted by not just five-star hotels and restaurants but by many shops and hotels with a less affluent clientele. You will, however, still be hard-pressed to find a familiar credit card sticker on a merchant's door deep in the rural heartland of any developing country.

Of all the cards available, the major three — MasterCard, Visa and American Express — are your best bet for general worldwide acceptance. They usually require that you obtain gold card status before any real travel benefits can be enjoyed. Although you should check with your banking institution regarding the most current program benefits, some may include overall life and (limited) health insurance, pre-trip cancellation, trip interruption insurance (medical), delayed or lost baggage protection, collision coverage for rental cars, souvenir or purchase protection and transport bankruptcy protection. American Express membership offers most of these advantages and more. With over 1,700 offices worldwide, it boasts by far the most exposure and respectability. American Express membership offers the traveler a few more unique and very useful services:

☐ Unlimited charging capabilities, which can be handy during emergencies such as paying for expensive vehicle repairs or airline tickets.

☐ Personal checking privileges for up to US$1,000 worth of traveler's checks with an Amex green card and up to US$5,000 with a gold card every twenty-one days. This benefit circumvents the mountain of bureaucratic and logistical problems involved in wiring funds from home.

☐ The use of American Express facilities for mail drops and message pickups. Some locations even have phone and fax facilities.

☐ A medical and legal reference hot line.

☐ The strength and visibility of a credit card that implies to most foreign officials (whether true or not) that, yes, you are a somebody! (And once again, this is not an advertisement.)

A credit card is one of the most valuable and yet most vulnerable of your important travel documents. You should protect it as you would your cash, passport, vaccination card and plane ticket. A lost credit card can come back to haunt you if the loss is not reported quickly and properly.

TIPS FOR TRIPS

- Photocopy your credit card, keeping one copy with you and another at home.

- Check with the issuing bank about exact benefits and service charges.

- Make sure you know whether exchange is calculated on the day of the transaction or the day of processing.

- If you are an American Express cardholder with the ability to draw personal checks and large sums of money every twenty-one days, attempt to negotiate an arrangement with American Express that will make it difficult to draw those funds unless certain prearranged criteria are met, such as a phone call for authorization. This will prevent abuse of your card in cases of extortion or shakedowns.

- Keep receipts for all purchases.

- Keep in contact with the person who is paying your credit card bills for you back at home. This ensures that any irregularities are caught before too long and do not have to be explained and recovered at a later date.

- Purchases of airline tickets, rental cars, breakable purchases and so on may be insured if paid for with your credit card. Check with the card issuer for details.

- When merchants are making an imprint, watch carefully to prevent them from making a few extra.

- If you must leave your card stored in a secure place for any reason or for any amount of time, take care to make it unnoticeable or inaccessible. Cards have often been used to charge up items while the owner was out of town trekking or river rafting. The cardholder will have no knowledge of the abuse until receipt of the statement.

- Always report a lost or stolen card immediately.

- If you are a credit cardholder on an extended trip, never let the credit card company know you are unemployed. Some cardholders have had their cards revoked when they attempted to get a cash advance. They had made the mistake of declaring on the request form that they were unemployed while traveling.

I was in French Polynesia, sick with dengue fever. I was not staying in the best of accommodations. In fact, I was sharing a room with cockroaches, mosquitos and rats. It was so hot I couldn't stop sweating, and since there was no shower, feeling clean was out of the question. I was miserable but didn't have the strength or available cash to do anything about it.

I made my way to the phone and managed to call my mom at home. When I told her of my predicament she answered as only a mother could: "You have no cash, but you do have that Visa card, don't you? Well that's what it's for. So use it and get yourself to a place where you can heal!" I don't know why I didn't think of it. I moved to a nice hotel, where my first words were, "I want a room and I want to charge it on my Visa!" Thanks to my credit card, I got a great room and recovered quickly. – CARYL

Money Transfers

If your trip promises to outlast your immediate money supply, you must make arrangements to replenish it. This is an area where travel anxiety rates high, since the only reason you are sending home for money is because your current reserves are dwindling. The fact that you have gotten the wheels rolling long before your money ran out is of little comfort when it is overdue by a week or two (or worse). The main problem with receiving funds from home is not only bureaucratic red tape, or the high possibility of incompetence and honest human error, but the occassional sheer greed of the institutions involved. Third world banks make interest on all hard currency held in their system, so in some cases they will hold on to your transfer as long as possible. Good business for them, but a nightmare for you.

Solution? Stay away from money transfers as much as possible. If you must transfer money be prepared to harass and hang around.

TIPS FOR TRIPS

- Make sure beforehand that money will be issued in traveler's checks or hard currency.

- Try to use a common bank that has headquarters or branches in your own country such as Bank of America, Royal Bank, Barclays and City Bank.

- Keep track of the names of appropriate people involved and bank addresses or numbers.

- Make sure money is cabled or telexed, never mailed.

- It's possible that your money may go to another bank by mistake, so stay in touch with the sender for unfolding details.

- Again, be prepared to hassle, harass and hang around.

Options better than money transfers include

- Using Western Union for a reasonable fee but first making sure you can receive your funds in hard currency.

- Using your American Express card to write a personal check.

- Using your credit card for a cash advance. Keep in mind that interest on a cash advance accumulates from the day you receive the funds. Draw cash with your credit card and have your contact at home pay for it immediately. If your credit card gives you access to automated teller machines, you can draw funds directly in locations equipped with an ATM.

- Using a bank debit card to draw funds directly from your account back home.

However, discuss this option with your bank before leaving, and always show great caution when drawing money from an ATM, especially late at night.

◪ Purchasing traveler's checks before you leave and having someone document courier them to you with Federal Express, DHL, Purolator or any other worldwide courier company. Do not declare them as valuables but as documents because it is against company policy to carry the burden of responsibility for monetary items. In many third world countries there is a possibility that the package will be opened in one of their local offices or in transit, rifled for anything of value and resealed or put in a new envelope. If that happens, just receive the package, check its contents and if the checks are there, smile and leave. If not, complain to the company for their lack of security, get a refund on your courier cost, then go to your traveler's check office and apply there for the refund of your stolen checks.

◪ It hardly needs to be said, but never send cash via courier.

Vaccination Cards

Once you know your destination, visit your local board of health or medical clinic. Let them know your itinerary so they can offer you immunization information and vaccinations. It is wise to start the program as soon as possible because some vaccinations consist of a series of shots over a period of time. It's best to get all shots from one clinic rather than finishing them on the road. Vaccinations in third world countries can be a hassle and costly, but more importantly, with the very real threat of AIDS, they can be dangerous as well. Another consideration is the possibility of a reaction to a vaccination. You could come down with a short but intense illness while your body builds an immunity. If this occurs, you want it to happen well in advance of your departure date.

When you receive your shots, you should be given a certificate or record book as proof of your vaccination. This proof is a permanent record to be kept safely in your passport pouch at all times. The vaccination record is not only important when entering a foreign country. It also is vital information for you and the immunization nurse about the status of your vaccinations and will help identify your need for supplementary vaccinations or booster shots.

With the eradication of many diseases around the world, proof of vaccination is required less frequently. However, if and when the need arises, it is very important to be able to produce such a document. Without it the authorities may want to administer the shots in question on their own terms, and this opens the door to a whole host of new problems. Although the World Health Organization is making great headway in the area of disease control, many diseases are coming back with a vengeance. The day when all travelers will need to present their cards on a regular basis may soon return.

Other Medical Concerns

Once your shots are out of the way, take a trip to your doctor and dentist and explain your plans. Along with providing advice, he or she may help you in gathering some valuable supplies to stock your medical kit. These may include prescriptions for ailments, allergies and malaria pills; codeine tablets or cough syrup; antibiotics and so forth. Your medical kit should also contain a card with blood type information and any personal health concerns.

It is important to remember that if you have permanent health condition or allergies, you should wear a medic alert bracelet or some form of identification that provides vital medical information in case you become incapacitated.

If health matters are serious concern for you, you may consider becoming a member of the International Association for Medical Assistance to Travelers (IAMAT), which issues health information for overseas travel and provides a complete listing of English- and French-speaking doctors around the world:

United States
736 Center Street
Lewiston, New York, 14092
Phone (716) 754-4883

Canada
40 Regal Road
Guelph, Ontario, N1K 1B5
Phone (416) 652-0137
Fax (519) 836-3412

Dental Concerns

Do not make the mistake of leaving home without a complete dental checkup. Just because your teeth are fine at home doesn't mean they won't attempt a revolt a few months down the road. If you talk to anyone who has had to seek dental work during a trip, you will understand that it is not always a pleasant experience.

TIPS FOR TRIPS

- Stay away from rock-hard food.
- Follow a regular routine of dental hygiene.
- Refrain from foolish behavior like opening bottles with teeth.
- Carry clove oil or Ambesol for reducing toothaches in an emergency.

DOCUMENT SECURITY

The minute you leave home, your passport, money and plane ticket are by far the most valuable items in your world. Treat them accordingly. To make sure they are kept safe and accessible, you will have to keep them in a secure place on your person. The options include a passport waist pouch, shoulder pouch, belt pouch or compartments sewn inside your clothing. Each is secure in its own way but also is vulnerable to some degree. As a final security measure

you should create a duplicate home file, where copies of
your most important documents are stored.

Passport Waist Pouch

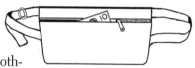

A passport waist pouch
has more than sufficient
room for personal docu-
ments, can be worn under cloth-
ing and is readily accessible, though it may take some time
for you to get used to having it around your waist. During
the first segment of any long hot trip, expect some discomfort. Friction combined with sweat will rub the first few layers of tan off your lower belly beneath the belt. Sliding it
around to your back may relieve some of the pressure, but
it's not a good practice to wear your valuables behind you.
In time, as you become more accustomed to the belt, you
probably won't even notice it, and the bulge created will
more than likely become comfortably reassuring over time.

Passport Shoulder Pouch

A passport shoulder pouch is worn around
your neck, lying flat on the chest, stomach
or under your arm. It is comfortable, practical for travel and accessible. It keeps
your valuables out of view and safe from
being compressed as they would be in
the waist pouch. But the drawback is
that the string around your neck can
be broken with enough effort or skill.
Grab-and-run thefts also are quite common during the brief
moments when it is out in the open. Piano wire or a sturdy
guitar string sewn into the strap around your neck will make
it far more secure, though it might prove painful if someone
attempts to pull it off.

Passport Belt Pouch

A passport belt pouch is a popular form of document protection. It's a sturdy leather pouch that looks something like a flat holster worn on the front side of your hip. The pouch is just big enough to hold your important documents snugly inside. It is attached to your belt, and its opening is secured by a buckle. Velcro sewn to the strap makes it next to impossible for someone to lift the strap through the buckle without detection. The pouch should be attached by two secure points, whether they are separate belt loops or an additional thin wire around the waist. The heavy leather makes it difficult (though not impossible) to cut.

It's advantages are that it's comfortable, durable and accessible. With an add-on strap or string, it can also be worn around your neck and under your shirt. The belt pouch, however, has two drawbacks. First, it is not waterproof. Though your documents will be in plastic, the pouch can get wet, causing the dye in the leather to run. Second, because it is usually worn on the outside of your clothing, it's quite visible. If this makes you uncomfortable, wear a long shirt over your pouch or shift it from your side to the front of your waist.

Compartments Sewn Inside Clothing

Compartments sewn inside clothing are probably the best way of concealing your valuables. But any self-respecting thief knows that anyway. With enough skill and determination a thief will be able to locate and extricate your valuables, either by force or cunning.

Clothing compartments are not very practical because of the sheer weight of your documents pressing into your groin or rubbing on the inside of your leg. It's also difficult to get to your valuables quickly and discretely, and unless you always wear the same clothing you will have to sew pockets into your entire travel wardrobe. Nevertheless, we've met many travelers who swear that this method is worth the hassle.

TIPS FOR TRIPS

- Have photocopies of all your important documents in the event of loss or theft. Replacing them is usually not a big deal, but time is the all-important factor. The better you are able to provide necessary information, the faster the appropriate authorities will be able to replace what has gone missing. This information can be sent by fax or phone. Keep photocopies separate from your valuables. If traveling with a partner, it is a good idea to carry photocopies of the other person's documents in the event that only one of you is relieved of your possessions.

- Storing your documents in a plastic bag is essential to keep them free from humidity, sweat and rain. A Ziplock baggie is good, but it is also important to have quick, unencumbered access in tight or unsecured circumstances.

- To secure straps on money pouches and shoulder bags, Velcro or heavy wire (piano or a bass guitar string) works great. Just make sure it is sewn in properly to protect you from any harm if it is pulled quickly and with force.

- Most importantly, protect your documents at all costs! Never let your guard down. Take them to the toilet and the shower. If neccessary sleep with your pouch tied to your wrist, or under your pillow or head. You will eventually learn through time and experience when it is safe to let your guard down. Until then, it is better to err on the side of safety.

- Hotel safes are not always secure but will do in a pinch if you are confident of the staff and circumstances. Make sure the safe is secure, count and itemize everything in your packet (in the presence of a hotel representative) and always get a signed receipt.

Duplicate Home File

Leave a copy of your travel documents at home in a safe place and make it accessible to a designated person who will be attending to your affairs while you're away. This file should contain

☐ Three photocopies of all items in your document pouch: one for your file at home, one for your passport pouch and one as a backup in your travel bag.

☐ Traveler's check numbers.

☐ Bank account and credit card numbers.

☐ Will and living will.

☐ Power of attorney for bank accounts and for the guardian watching your children (or pets), giving them permission to sign for emergency surgery or medical treatment.

☐ Copies of life, property and health insurance.

☐ Medical history, including medications, allergies, blood type and RH factor.

☐ Doctor's phone number and your health plan number.

BAGGAGE

Before packing you will have to decide what form of bag best suits your needs. For long-term budget travel there are only two options to consider: a backpack (internal or external frame) and a shoulder or duffle bag.

Backpack

Backpacks are of two types: top-loading, which has a string to close the bag, and front-loading, which has zippers around the bag. Top-loaders are generally for actual hiking or mountaineering and have great back support. Front-loaders are for carrying your gear from the station to your hotel, where it will stay the majority of time. These bags lack back support, but because you're not in the mountains climbing for hours on end, you won't need an extra cushion.

The other difference between these types of bags is the ability to get what you need quickly. With top-loaders, access to items on the bottom is difficult without a long arm and a willingness to search blindly. Front-loading bags can be quickly opened, exposing all their contents.

All backpacks come with internal or external frames. External frames are better suited to long treks because they allow you to strap on much more weight. But unlike packs with internal frames, external frames pose hassles when moving through crowds and tight places, and they can't be compressed for travel. On the overland trail you are constantly moving, taking various forms of transportation on a regular basis, so a bag with an internal frame is a better, more adaptable overall design for travel.

A well-made, properly adjusted backpack allows you to walk great distances without overburdening you with uneven weight distribution. Its disadvantages are its vulnerability to theft (with its many outside pockets) and the way it labels you as a traveler in crowds. Although attitudes toward backpacking "hippie" travelers have changed dramatically since the seventies, a stigma remains. All that aside, the backpack is still the most realistic means of packing for overland travel.

Tips for Trips

- When buying a backpack, spend a little more money to get a well-built product that will stand the test of overland travel. Check seams and straps for strength. Coated nylon will make the pack much more water resistant.

- When checking your pack for transport on a bus, train or plane, make sure all straps and buckles are secure to reduce the chance of anything getting snagged or ripped. On airplanes you might be able to put your pack in a large plastic bag, which will be tied at the top. Airlines aren't likely to compensate for a damaged backpack. Inquire about their policy ahead of time if you have any concerns.

- Excess straps, too common on modern packs, should be cut off and the nylon ends sewn (hemmed) or melted with a lighter or match.

- All pockets should be secured or locked with small key or combination locks to discourage theft.

- In damp, dirty or dusty environments, a pack cover is highly recommended. It protects the pack from the elements, not to mention covert attempts at entry. You can buy covers ready-made, make one yourself before leaving or improvise with a large burlap sack used for packing flour or rice.

- Buy a pack that gives you access to different levels of contents and that has only one large or a few outside pockets.

- Make sure your pack is adjusted to your specific body size and weight. A poorly adjusted backpack can be a real liability on the road.

If growth occurs during times of adversity, then losing your backpack thousands of miles away from home can be a glorious opportunity for personal progress! I have certainly met people who have had this experience, and some have looked at their loss as an opportunity to truly liberate themselves from the preoccupation of constantly protecting their possessions. They accepted the fact that nothing could be done but to make plans to head home or restock and move along.

Nothing should be carried in your pack that can't easily be replaced with little expense. What can't be replaced should be securely carried on your person.
– WAYNE

Shoulder Bag

Although a duffle bag is not as practical as a backpack for walking, it is easier to work with when in transit, offers better accessibility to contents and is less conspicuous in large groups of luggage.

TIPS FOR TRIPS

- Make sure it has hand straps that run completely around the bottom of the bag for support and one long adjustable shoulder strap running end to end.

- Sturdy canvas or Cordura is preferable to nylon because it is more durable and difficult to rip or slash.

- A dark color will camouflage dirt and stains.

- A heavy-duty metal zipper with a lock ring on the end is essential for security and longevity.

Backpack in Repose

Flag (torn and frayed).

Maps, photos, socks, undies, sweaters, bedroll, shorts, jacket, art supplies, guidebooks, novel, postcards, stamps, snacks and lint!

Toothpaste, toothbrush, comb, cup, scissors, tableware, photo film, plastic bags, souvenir ashtray, etc., etc.

Bar of soap, shampoo, suntan cream, burn ointment and Kaopectate (large).

No guns, dope or dirty postcards.

Pins and needles, gauze, aspirin, tape, malaria pills, antiseptic, thread, nylon chord and a partridge in a pear tree!

PACKING

On a long journey even a straw weighs heavy.
– SPANISH PROVERB

The cardinal rule of packing is to pack what you think you will need and then take half out! Pack according to the climates you will encounter and the activities you will take part in. Consider as well that many things are available and cheaper overseas or in developing countries, depending on where you go. After deciding what to bring you will have to consider the best way to pack it all.

Packing Suggestions

Clothing

☐ A sturdy pair of hiking boots or walking shoes. These are probably your most important purchase for an extended overland journey. Remember to balance durability and comfort with weight.

☐ Sandals or thongs. Before leaving home, get rubber flip-flops, or sandals of good quality, and a backup pair if possible. These will be worn not only on the beach but on bathroom floors, in shower stalls, in hotel rooms or in places where fungal infections may be a concern.

☐ Underwear.

☐ Light undershirt (good for protecting your skin from coarse blankets in cooler regions).

☐ Several cotton shirts. Refrain from packing clothing that is military green or could be confused with army issue.

☐ Several pairs of pants. Light cotton is best for warmer climates. Jeans are fine for cooler climates but can be heavy and take a long time to wash and dry.

☐ Several pairs of socks comfortable for hiking or those long days on your feet.

☐ A couple of pairs of shorts (sturdy and dark are best).

☐ Belt.

☐ Sweater.

☐ Swimsuit.

☐ Light waterproof jacket.

☐ Rain jacket or poncho that will cover both you and your pack.

☐ Sarong or cotton wrap (easier to use on the beach than a sandy or soggy towel).

☐ Durable hat that can withstand sun and rain.

☐ Sunglasses. Good quality and fit are far more important than looks.

☐ Cotton handkerchief.

☐ Sleeping shirt or pajamas.

Toiletries and Towels

☐ Tweezers.

☐ Nail clippers.

☐ Brush and comb.

☐ Soap.

☐ Stick deodorant.

☐ Razor.

☐ Toothbrush, toothpaste, dental floss.

☐ Unbreakable mirror.

☐ Tiger balm for sore muscles.

☐ Tampons. Plenty of pads are usually available but tampons are next to unheard-of outside large third world cities.

☐ Toilet paper. (Take the cardboard roll out of the center and compress.)

☐ Skin lotion with sunscreen.

☐ Lip balm with sunscreen.

☐ Visine or similar eye-care product for sore, tired or red eyes.

☐ Sunscreen. Those available overseas may not offer different levels of sun protection.

☐ Baby powder (optional).

☐ Ear swabs.

☐ Towel. You can now purchase thin, lightweight muslin towels that are very absorbant and can be wrung out to dry quickly. Towels made with a heavy pile are bulky and take far too long to dry. Purchasing a large towel and cutting it in half will ensure you always have one that is dry.

Medical Kit

☐ Codeine tablets for pain relief. Keep a copy of the prescription (if required). Also pack over-the-counter headache tablets such as Tylenol or Aspirin.

☐ Malaria pills (if needed).

☐ Antibiotics and prescription medications. Many doctors advise you not to treat yourself, but antibiotics do come in handy. Find out as much about them from your doctor as possible beforehand! If you need a steady supply of any prescription medication, pack enough to last the duration of your trip. Keep medication in its original container. Pack medications in an airtight box or bag away from contaminants and humidity. Pharmacies in developing countries are woefully understocked, and if by chance they do carry the medication you need, it may be adulterated or long past its expiration date. Also, keep in mind that other countries may market the same drugs under different names.

☐ Band-Aids.

☐ Hydrogen peroxide for disinfecting cuts and scrapes.

☐ Antihistamines for insect bites and allergies. If you are

allergic to bee stings remember to carry an anti-venom kit.

☐ Cold remedies and cough syrup. (Tropical colds are the worst!)

☐ Water purification chemicals or tablets. Iodine works well but can be messy. Keep it in a leakproof container.

☐ Preparation H if needed. Suppositories will melt in hot and humid conditions.

☐ Antacids for heartburn and the aftereffects of spicy foods.

☐ Mosquito repellent. (Look for the active ingredient, DEET, which should be labeled no more than 50 percent. Be careful of potential allergic reactions when using products containing DEET.)

☐ Antibacterial cream.

☐ Anti-fungal cream or powder.

☐ Clove oil for toothaches.

☐ Thermometer.

☐ Contraceptives.

General Items

☐ Passport photos (for visa and gift exchanges). Automatic photo booths in airports provide a good, cheap backup.

☐ If you will be doing any amount of driving while away, you should get an international driver's license and insurance.

☐ Photo of spouse and children (whether you have them or not) to be used at appropriate times for respectability.

☐ Wedding ring for singles who do not want unsolicited advances from members of the opposite sex.

☐ Camera, good supply of film and extra batteries.

- ☐ Combination or key locks. Essential for hotel rooms and bags.
- ☐ A good map of the country or countries you will be traveling through.
- ☐ Key ring.
- ☐ Rubber doorstop and bells on a string (to be attached to door at night to warn you of intruders).
- ☐ Lighters. Third world matches are a fire hazard and should always be struck away from you.
- ☐ Earplugs for sleeping in noisy locations.
- ☐ Eye covers for sleep in lighted situations.
- ☐ Plastic cup.
- ☐ Knife, spoon and fork kit. Swiss Army knife is the most versatile.
- ☐ Stationery and writing material.
- ☐ Patches, pins and mini-flags (great presents for hospitality and easy to carry).
- ☐ Clothespins and laundry line.
- ☐ Day pack or bag.
- ☐ Flashlight with backup bulb.
- ☐ Sewing kit. (Best to learn a little about sewing before you leave.)
- ☐ Water bottle.
- ☐ Post-It notes.
- ☐ Travel alarm clock.
- ☐ Batteries. Third world batteries are cheap but notorious for poor quality, so it's important to have a reasonable supply of backup batteries for your alarm clock, flash-

light and so on. Also, good travel etiquette requires you to provide your own power source while listening to someone else's Walkman.

☐ Portable CD or tape player and discs or tapes (if desired).

☐ A watch that you wouldn't mind losing or breaking.

☐ Security bag or plastic containers to protect food and toiletries from elements and insects.

☐ Brightly colored marker or a highlighting pen for marking information in your travel guide, books, notices and so forth.

☐ Black felt pen with indelible ink for shipping, clothes identification and so on.

☐ Cellophane tape for ripped maps, books, money and so on.

☐ Velcro, fabric glue or Crazy Glue for repairs.

☐ Sleeping bag (optional). A youth hostel sleeping sheet is more practical in warmer climates.

☐ Foam pad (optional).

☐ Compass (optional).

☐ Drain stopper plug (one-size-fits-all variety).

☐ Pillowcase to stuff and make a pillow or to replace soiled ones in cheap hotels.

☐ Three small record keepers: an address book (remember to keep a separate copy of the most important names and addresses), a small diary to record expenses and keep you on budget, and a small notebook with detachable pages for sketching—a picture *is* worth a thousand words, especially to cab drivers or shopkeepers who may not speak your language.

☐ You will be swamped with pieces of paper—business cards, phone numbers, mementos and so on. Many will be important, so quick reference is a must. A durable plastic folder, envelope or bag will keep everything organized.

☐ A personal journal, preferably hardcover for recording those not-to-be-forgotten events. Throughout the years such journals will become as important as your photographs.

☐ Candles for the power outages common in third world countries. Candles are always cheaper abroad.

☐ Incense (if desired).

☐ Backup eyeglasses. If you are dependent upon glasses, it is wise to carry an extra pair. They should be carried in a durable case. Also carry a copy of your prescription. In some countries such as India you can have uncomplicated prescriptions filled quite easily for a fraction of the cost at home. Do not consider wearing contact lenses. They are very susceptible to dust, and it will be next to impossible to keep them sterilized.

☐ Games for diversion or pastimes. Keep them small and simple. Miniature cards, backgammon, chess and hackey sack are travel favorites. Also, practice a little volleyball before you leave. This, along with board and card games, provides entertainment on the overland trail.

☐ Combination lock and bike cable to secure your luggage.

☐ Finally, a good book—preferably one that provides insight into the culture through which you are traveling. Barring that, bring something trashy for a complete escape.

Before trading a book to another traveler, write on the inside cover your name, the date and the country you were traveling through. In the early eighties, while traveling through Southeast Asia, I read W. Harbinson's Genesis. When finished, I traded it for another book and kicked myself for years after for having done so. It had gone out of print, and I could not find another copy anywhere. Then, when I returned to northern Thailand in 1993, I bought the same book at a used bookstore. Owners' names and destinations scrawled within the covers would have made the experience of recovering the book even more rewarding. If it was my original copy, it had probably had a most interesting ten-year journey. – WAYNE

TIPS FOR TRIPS

- Some people would rather travel heavy than go without, but we caution you to travel with only what you can comfortably carry.

- In many countries you can have travel clothing made that will not only be inexpensive but durable enough to become a momento of your travels.

- Items in your pack can be retrieved quicker if they're always stored in the same place.

- Pack breakables and hard articles in the middle, wrapped or surrounded by soft things. Any liquid container that may be broken during transit should be packed in plastic.

- For best use of space, roll clothes instead of folding them.

- Don't bury your toiletries. Keep them accessible by packing them near the top.

- Make sure your clock or flashlight will not be activated in transit, burning out batteries and causing a general nuisance. Taking the batteries out or turning them around will insure the appliance will not be accidentally turned on.

- Airline safety regulations require you to pack all knives and dangerous material in checked luggage.

- Excess baggage charges can be quite expensive, so keep the number of bags to a minimum, usually your pack and one piece of hand luggage.

- Keep all toiletries, a change of clothes and valuables in hand luggage or a shoulder bag to hold you over if your backpack goes missing.

- Never pack anything irreplaceable.

Physical Health

Overall, world health conditions are slowly improving, but the same cannot be said for the third world. Realistically speaking, your exposure to unfamiliar, unhealthy surroundings increases your risk of getting sick, especially with stomach ailments. There is no need to become paranoid, but you will inevitably become ill some time along the way. Statistics show that if you take care of yourself and take some commonsense precautions, the chances of becoming seriously ill are greatly reduced. Food, water, insects, altitude and attitude can all be sources of disease or discomfort. Your destination guidebook should fill you in on the overall range of health-related difficulties that you might encounter in a particular country. More than likely, however, few (if any) will be a concern. Overland budget travelers should take special care to avoid the following common complaints and illnesses.

PREVENTATIVE HEALTH MEASURES

TIPS FOR TRIPS

- Stay away from ice and ice cream.
- Eat only fruit and vegetables that can be boiled, peeled or cleaned with purified water.
- Watch how waiters and cooks grab straws from straw containers for your

drinks. Drink out of the end that has not been touched by their fingers or get the straw yourself.

- ◪ To avoid the risk of catching hepatitis or other infectious diseases, do not drink from other people's bottles or glasses or share their cigarettes.

- ◪ Keeping your finger- and toenails cut short improves personal hygiene.

- ◪ Remember that everything from handrails to coins carries the legacy of past handlers. Keep your fingers out of your mouth and don't chew on pens.

- ◪ Wash your hands frequently (without getting compulsive).

- ◪ Acclimatize yourself slowly to changes in altitude, temperature or any other severe environmental change.

- ◪ In hot and humid climates, take as many cool showers during the day as needed to keep you comfortable.

- ◪ If the heat and humidity of the lowlands is wearing you thin, consider a short period of physical and emotional relief by going to a hill station or the highlands, where the climate is much more pleasant.

- ◪ Massages relieve not just stiff and sore muscles but also the tension that sometimes goes with foreign travel. Massages are generally of two types. The first is gentle, loosens muscles and promotes relaxation immediately. The second is more aggressive and is meant to go deep into the muscles and tendons to release built-up toxins that create tension and stiffness. The benefits of deep massage are not realized until a few days later. Through the thin walls of cheap hotels, the gentle massage sounds like two people enjoying extended foreplay and the second sounds more like a mugging. Foot rubs are also a pleasant option.

- ◪ If you are feeling ill but must travel, choose a window seat for fresh air.

Indonesia is notorious for travelers with very weak stomachs. If you travel there, you are guaranteed to experience half of the people on the bus being sick. They are conditioned to throw up at their feet rather than in a bag or out the window. The vomit remains until the driver stops and gathers straw to throw on the mess so people can put their feet down without getting wet. – WAYNE

- Always wear something on your feet. Coming into contact with diseases like ringworm, athlete's foot and plantar warts is highly possible on streets, shower floors and even the beach. Footwear is also important for reducing the chances of cuts and punctures.

- Be careful when walking on the beach. Broken bottles, tabs from cans, shells or coral can cut your feet. If you see something sharp or dangerous, pick it up so the next person won't step on it, but be careful handling it.

- If a dog is barking at you, ignore it. If it begins to charge, face it, raise your arm as if you have a stick, or reach for a rock and look prepared to throw it. This is what most locals do. If an attacking dog has already latched on to your limb, do not attempt to pull it away. Instead, push your limb farther into the dog's mouth and it will eventually let it go. If that fails, punch the dog directly in the nose and seek medical treatment immediately! Always show caution around any animals, especially dogs, horses and monkeys.

My friends and I had just left our rented car and were walking through the parking lot when what seemed to be a giant-sized fur ball came flying out of nowhere and knocked me off balance. A monkey had just flung itself determinedly at my neck. I didn't realize what had happened until I saw the little beast tear off down the road with my newly purchased pair of Bollé sunglasses. He raced behind a barbed-wire fence, sat down and then nonchalantly began to gnaw on my glasses. I ran up to the fence and, feeling somewhat intimidated by the animal, began shouting insults and obscenities in a futile attempt to stir him to some kind of action.

At that point I recognized the absurdity of my folly. Before being pressed into a more realistic, confrontational action, a Balinese man walked up to the monkey and offered it some peanuts. In a second the monkey grabbed the peanuts and dropped my glasses.

– Valerie, Canada

61

CLIMATE AND HEALTH

Prickly Heat

Excessive perspiration trapped under the skin can turn into an itchy rash. It usually affects you only if you have just arrived in a hot, humid climate. The pores of your skin have not yet adjusted to the increased volume of sweat. If this happens, take comfort in knowing it is only temporary and can be treated effectively by washing or bathing often, using talcum powder, or if all else fails, relocating to a cooler environment.

Sunburn

Even on cloudy days you can get badly burned. In the tropics and at high altitudes, the sun can be very severe, and the accumulation of UV rays can affect you more quickly than you may be used to. Use sunscreen (SPF 15 to protect skin from UV rays), giving special attention to areas of your body which seldom are exposed to the sun (especially important when nude sunbathing because bare feet, bottoms and genitalia are particularly vulnerable). Remember that sunscreen must be put on half an hour before going into the sun for maximum effectiveness. Of course, much can be prevented by keeping covered and wearing a hat.

Heat Exhaustion

High temperatures and humidity cause the body to lose fluids through excessive sweating. If bodily fluids are not replenished, heat exhaustion can occur. Symptoms include fatigue, lethargy, headache, giddiness and muscle cramps. Treatment involves moving out of the heat and drinking enough liquids to return the body to its normal state. Dehydration can be treated with liquids, particularly those containing electrolytes. An effective home remedy can include one cup of boiled water flavored with lemon, lime or orange juice; a pinch of salt; and one teaspoon of sugar. Commercial rehydration solutions are sold at pharmacies and can be carried in your pack. Some common commercial names are Gastrolyte, Pedialyte and Rapolyte. Heat exhaustion can be avoided by wearing a sun hat and drinking plenty of liquids in hot weather.

Heatstroke

Heatstroke is a true medical emergency that can occur when heat exhaustion goes untreated. It is characterized by a high body temperature (39–41°C / 102–106°F) and a cessation of sweating. Symptoms are flushed red skin, headache and confusion, which may progress to delirium or convulsions if left untreated. At this point it is essential that someone help you get out of the sun and to a hospital for rehydration.

HYGIENE AND HEALTH

Traveler's Diarrhea

Undoubtedly you will fall victim to traveler's diarrhea at some time during your travels. To be fair, though, it is a problem you may as easily encounter at home. Diarrhea is typically caused by bacteria, parasites or viruses entering the body in contaminated food or water, but it can occur for any number of reasons, including, quite simply, climate change and the stress it brings.

Human stomachs and intestines are host to a natural bacteria that break down and digest food. When moving from one location to another, you introduce new bacteria and your organs must readjust. During that period, you may feel symptoms of gas, upset stomach and runny stools. As many as six rushed visits to the toilet a day is not uncommon. Luckily, traveler's diarrhea is seldom a serious concern. Usually it will disappear within a few days, and until then you can take heart in knowing that it will help reduce your susceptibility to future upsets.

Diarrhea caused by contaminated food or water can result in more severe symptoms, ranging from mild stomach irritation or nausea to gut-wrenching pain. Your body is attempting to expel the bacteria responsible for its irritation.

There is not much you can do except rest as much as you can, increase your liquid intake to counter dehydration and wait for the plumbing to settle down and behave as it should. Drink weak black tea, flat soft drinks and purified or boiled water. Adding sugar will help the gut absorb more minerals. Eat only bland, basic food such as rice, dry bread and boiled eggs. Be very careful when using over-the-counter medication to treat diarrhea. Many, like Lomotil or Imodium, may relieve your symptoms, but they can also stop you up, denying your body an avenue for expelling the guilty bacteria. Rest and time are always the best ways to treat diarrhea.

Lome, the capital of Togo, is a free port on the Gulf of Guinea and a Mecca of western goods and indulgences. After weeks of desert deprivations I pigged out on pizza, steak, ice cream and beer. While sitting outside the central police station awaiting movement on the wheels of visa bureaucracy, my body rebelled. I felt not just the call but the shriek of nature. Across the road a derelict

*train yard seemed as inviting a lavatory as any in my
dire condition. There was no real cover and the yard was
suddenly full of Africans, some making their homes in
the unused boxcars. Committed and in desperation I
squatted in the fluted stalls of a Baobab tree trunk. The
locals were amused. I hunched, wracked by cramps,
while they roared for an encore. Pants to my knees I was
about to oblige when a frantic waving from the building
across the street caught my eye.*

*Upping my pants, I hobbled over. They bade me
enter. "Vite! Vite!" (Hurry! Hurry!) was their courteous
cry. I could barely follow my Samaritans on their jack-
rabbit run through the twisting corridors. A key turned
on some bureaucratic privy. The relief was enormous. I
returned to the steps of the building, where a small
crowd cheered and I acknowledged them with a sweaty
smile and wan wave as if I had just finished laying a
ceremonial cornerstone. We were at the* Ministere des
Affaires Etranges. *A strange affair indeed!*
– TONY JENKINS, *TRAVELLERS TALES*

Dysentery

When symptoms of diarrhea persist or get worse—
including long-term stomach cramps, nausea, blood or
mucus in the stools, burps which taste strongly of sulfur—
you may have bacillary dysentery or a variation called amoebic dysentery. Dysentery is not uncommon and is usually
cured in a relatively short time. But if left untreated, it
could easily turn into a serious or even life-threatening ailment. If blood is present in stools for a prolonged period,
seek medical attention immediately.

Bacillary dysentery is characterized by a high fever and
rapid development of headaches. Vomiting and stomach
pains are also symptoms. It generally does not last longer

than a week, but it is highly contagious. The prescribed treatment for this kind of dysentery is tetracycline.

Amoebic dysentery develops gradually without the symptoms of fever or vomiting, but it is a far more serious illness. It is not a self-limiting disease, and it will persist until treated. It can recur with the possibility of long-term damage. A stool test is necessary to diagnose which form of dysentery you have. So if you are concerned, seek medical help. In case of emergency, the prescribed treatment for amoebic dysentery is metronidazole.

Hepatitis

Hepatitis A (infectious hepatitis) is spread by contaminated food and water, and is far more common than Hepatitis B (serum hepatitis), which is spread through sexual contact or skin penetration. The first symptoms of both forms are fevers, chills, headaches, fatigue, weakness, aches and pains. After that, expect a loss of appetite, nausea, vomiting, abdominal pain, dark urine, light-colored feces and jaundiced skin (the whites of the eyes also may turn yellow). In milder cases there may simply be a general feeling of unwellness or fatigue accompanied by a loss of appetite, aches, pains and jaundice. Medical advice should be sought, but in general there is not much you can do apart from resting, drinking plenty of fluids, eating lightly and avoiding fatty foods. After a case of hepatitis you must refrain from drinking alcohol for six months, as hepatitis attacks the liver, which needs at least that amount of time to recover. A very effective Hepatitis A vaccine has recently been made available, and if you are venturing to places where Hepatitis A is a concern, it should be included in your series of pre-trip vaccination shots.

Hepatitis B is spread through sexual contact or skin penetration (dirty needles, accidental pricking, cuts and so on). Because type B is spread through sexual contact or skin penetration, you should avoid body piercing, tattooing, acupuncture or injections of any kind in unsanitary conditions. Sexual contact without condoms is playing Russian roulette at the best of times, but even more dangerous in countries where Hepatitis B is prevalent, which includes much of the Pacific Rim. The symptoms and treatment of Hepatitis B are much the same as for type A. A highly effective vaccine is readily available in most developed countries.

Bilharzia

Bilharzia is a common parasitic disease in Africa caused by blood flukes (minute worms) and requires immediate medical attention. Human infection can follow contact with the parasite in rivers and lakes, especially slow-moving or stagnant water. The parasite penetrates the skin, matures and then multiplies in various organs of the body. The infection begins as an itchy rash where the parasite initially penetrates the skin. If it migrates in the blood to the body's organs, it will cause persistent and cumulative damage by depositing its eggs, which begins a destructive reproductive cycle. A parasite laying eggs in the colon, for example, causes pain and blood in the feces, while an infected liver causes abdominal pain.

To avoid bilharzia, stay out of rivers and lakes that may be contaminated, and if you drink water from any of these sources, sterilize it with chlorine tablets or by boiling. The snail hosts favor shallow water near the shores of lakes and streams, and are more abundant where water polluted by human excrement is prevalent. Generally speaking, moving water presents less risk of infection than stagnant water, but you can never be sure so be careful. Because the snails live only in fresh water, there is no chance of catching bilharzia in the sea.

Sexually Transmitted Diseases

Sexual contact with an infected partner spreads diseases such as HIV, hepatitis, chlamydia, herpes, gonorrhea and syphilis. Short of abstinence, using a condom is the only safe way to protect yourself. If you've had unprotected sexual contact with a partner you later suspect of being infected, seek medical attention immediately. If you notice common symptoms of sexually transmitted diseases such as sores, blisters or rashes around the genitals or a painful discharge while urinating, then you may have become infected. Treatments for gonorrhea and chlamydia are oral tablets. Syphilis is treated with an antibiotic injection. If you must be treated for a sexually transmitted disease in a foreign country, be aware that disposable needles may have been resurrected from hospital waste bins.

Malaria

Malaria is a parasitic infection spread by the female *Anopheles* mosquito as it feeds on human blood. There is an eight- to thirty-day incubation period. The parasites invade the liver, using it as a staging area to attack red blood cells. After several days of development in the liver, immature parasites are released into the red blood cells. There, the parasites mature and enter the bloodstream to start the whole process over again. While this is taking place, you begin to feel the first symptoms, which subtly arise over a twenty-four–hour period and gradually become more frequent and severe. You suffer from high fever, chills and a general feeling of unwellness. Attacks can last up to eight hours. Nausea and vomiting also may occur. These episodes are usually followed by deep sleep and then by a flare up of symptoms as more parasites are released from the red blood cells. If you experience shivering, fever and a feeling of unwellness every forty-eight to seventy-two hours, seek medical attention.

Sound scary? It is. But in the world of travel, many people who have spent a great deal of time in the tropics have come down with the illness so many times that they now view it as casually as a cold or flu. This, however, is no reason to take the disease lightly.

The malaria risk currently is highest in sub-Saharan Africa and India. In Southeast Asia and Latin America, malaria typically is of concern only in remote rural areas. The risk in any country will vary with local conditions, such as mosquito control programs, time of year, weather and altitude, so it's wise to check malaria risk shortly before or upon arrival. Your best overall protection is always reducing your exposure and a proper prophylaxis program.

Tips for Trips

- Wear long-sleeved shirts and pants after dusk, when the malaria mosquitos become active.
- Use insect repellent containing DEET (30–50 percent).
- Make an effort to clear your room of mosquitoes before going to sleep.
- Make use of mosquito coils and netting.

Travelers to tropical countries should consult their doctor about the latest and most effective measures in the prevention and treatment of malaria. Children and pregnant and breast-feeding women are strongly advised to seek medical advice before traveling. Common treatments include

Chloroquine

Chloroquine-resistant strains of malaria have become so common around the world that generally Chloroquine is used only in combination with other drugs. It also may be substituted entirely with Mefloquine (Larium).

Program
– Adults take 1 (250 mg) tablet once a week or 1 (125 mg) tablet twice a week.
– Always take tablets on the same day or days each week.
– Start one week before entering a risk area and continue for four weeks after leaving.

Possible Side Effects
– Mild headaches.
– Itching.
– Dizziness.
– Minor stomach upsets, which can be reduced if pills are taken with a meal or in half doses twice a week.

Cautions
– Not recommended for children, pregnant women, breastfeeding women or people with liver disease, psoriasis, porphyria or severe seizure disorders.
– Overdoses may be fatal.

Mefloquine

Mefloquine is prescribed for travelers in areas with high chloriquine-resistant malarial strains. It is taken weekly, but can cause mild to severe side effects, so it should never be taken without medical advice.

Program
– Adults take 1 (250 mg) tablet with food and water once a week.
– Always take tablet on the same day each week.
– Start two weeks before entering risk a area and continue for four weeks after leaving.

Possible Side Effects
- Mild side effects, which occur in 25 percent of users, may include vivid dreams, nightmares, sleeping difficulty, loss of appetite, nausea, vomiting, dizziness and blurred vision, all of which become less severe as time passes.
- Moderate side effects, which occur in 1–2 percent of users, may include anxiety or panic attacks, depression, restlessness and confusion.
- Severe side effects, which occur in 1 in 12,000 users, may include convulsions, psychosis, hallucinations or paranoia.

Cautions
- Not recommended for people with a history of seizures, depression or psychiatric disorders; severe kidney, liver or heart disease; underlying cardiac conduction disturbances; or breast-feeding or pregnant women.

It is always recommended to seek medical advice when experiencing side effects from any medication.

Fansidar

No longer viewed as a safe preventative, fansidar is instead used as a treatment for malaria. Obviously, if you suspect you have malaria , proper medical attention should be sought immediately. Fansidar can, however, be carried in your medical kit as an emergency treatment when medical help is not readily available.

Program
- Adults take 3 (525 mg) tablets with water and food (stand-by treatment only).
- After first treatment, seek medical attention as soon as possible.

– Continue with regular program of anti-malarials.

Possible Side Effects
– Unlikely with single dose treatment.
– Allergic reactions such as itching, wheezing and hives.
– Feeling faint.

Cautions
– Not recommended for breast-feeding or pregnant women, babies under two months, people with sever liver problems or allergies to sulpha drugs.

Doxycycline

To be taken in daily 100-mg doses in the absence of a Chloriquine or Mefloquine program, or where strains are known to be resistant to either drug.

The first time I came down with malaria, I was with a friend in the Amazon. In the heat and humidity of the night, I slept in the nude, spread-eagled on some sorry excuse for a bed, trying to catch any stray movement of air for relief. I knew I was exposing myself to malaria-carrying mosquitos. But I was taking my chloroquine tablets faithfully, so what was there to worry about? Two weeks later I was sick with not one but two strains of malaria. My friend was not infected in the least. She had been using vast quantities of repellent, slipping into her sleeping bag and zipping it up over her head every night. To me this ritual seemed not only uncomfortable but impractical. Now I realize that protection is better obtained through reducing exposure than through prophylactics. – WAYNE

Cuts, Bites and Stings

Cuts and Scratches

Skin punctures can often become infected quickly in tropical climates and may take time and care to heal. Antiseptic solutions and creams or hydrogen peroxide will sterilize the area and promote healing. But try to leave the area exposed to air whenever possible by avoiding prolonged use of bandages or Band-Aids, which have a tendency to keep the wound moist.

Coral cuts are always slow to heal because of the weak venom injected into the wound. Avoid coral cuts by wearing shoes when walking or swimming near reefs. If you do cut yourself on the foot, keep it clean and dry. If necessary, place a sock over your foot and wear a sandal. Infections on the feet can be dangerous and are very slow to heal. A daily wash with hydrogen peroxide for the first while is also a good idea.

Bites and Stings

For most people, bee and wasp stings are usually more painful than dangerous. If you suffer from a bee sting, do not pull the stinger out with your fingers because the sack of venom is located at the base of the stinger. Any pressure will release more toxin into the skin. The stinger should be removed with a credit card or something flat and rigid. Slide it along the skin to scrape it out instead of pulling. Ice packs will reduce the swelling and relieve pain while rubbing aspirin or calamine lotion on the sting will neutralize the inflammatory agents in the venom. If you are allergic to aspirin, don't try rubbing it on your skin. You may also consider taking one tablet of antihistamine, such as chlortripolon (4 mg).

For some allergy sufferers, bee and wasp stings can be life-threatening. Breathing trouble, tightness in the chest and nausea are all signs of a serious allergic reaction. Areas of your body such as your neck may swell, cutting off the vital flow of air. People who know they are allergic should always carry a bee sting kit recommended by a physician. The kit will contain antihistamine pills and adrenaline injections. Remember that having a bee sting in the past without an allergic reaction does not ensure you will not acquire a sensitivity in the future, so it may be wise to carry a bee sting kit in any event.

Some protection from bees and other insects can be had by dressing in plain white or khaki. Avoid bright colors or strong floral patterns, and refrain from wearing sweet-smelling perfume and after-shave lotion.

In central Africa the greenery became claustrophobic. "It's a jungle out there." Days dawned almost prehistorically. Mists surrounded oversized foliage dappled with sunlight screened through the canopy of leaves thirty metres above. A strata of vines, ferns, mosses, creepers and tendrils competed for the light. The jungle floor was spongy and decayed. The shrieks of birds and monkeys echoed. Everything dripped with dew and hothouse life. A tyrannosaur would not have seemed amiss. The bug life was astounding. Again everything was oversized. The new creepy-crawly horrors of one night only became commonplace the next. I have only one rule: "Don't touch me!" They can come and go as they please but to crawl on me means instant squashing. A harsh law but I am outnumbered a billion to one! – TONY JENKINS, *TRAVELLERS TALES*

Bedbugs and Lice

Found mostly in dirty bedding and mattresses, bedbugs leave itchy bites in neat rows, which can be treated with calamine lotion. If you see spots of blood on bed clothes or on walls, chances are good that there are bedbugs around.

All lice cause itching and discomfort. They make themselves at home on your head (head lice), in your clothing (body lice) or in your pubic hair (crabs). The most likely way for you to catch lice is through direct contact with infected people or by sharing combs or clothing. Lice powder or a rinse called permethrin, available at most pharmacies or clinics, represents the best treatments. Wash infected clothing in very hot water.

Scorpions

Scorpions seek comfort in the cool and shade, which can include your shoes at night. Carefully shake out your shoes in the morning before putting them on.

Mosquitoes

Of all the insects you are likely to encounter, mosquitoes will probably be the most frequent annoyance. They buzz around your ears when you are trying to sleep and their bites are uncomfortable. As well, there is always the possibility of malaria or another mosquito-borne disease being transmitted. In some situations, avoiding mosquitos may be next to impossible, but you can always try to avoid being bitten. Before retiring for the night, attempt to clear your lodging of any of the pesky insects that slipped in during the day. Remember that they like to hide under things, in folds of clothing, bags, bedcovers and drapes, and in dark places.

If containment and control are difficult because of the nature of your accommodation, your next steps are covering with mosquito net, burning coils or using repellent.

Sleep with your body completely covered. If these measures fail, remember that excessive scratching can cause an infection that will be far worse than any mosquito bite. If your bites itch, use calamine lotion or rub the bite instead of scratching.

> *When I was in the jungle in Guatemala I decided not to wear mosquito spray in order to see how much damage they would actually do. I went to bed with mosquito coils burning in full force, believing I would be protected.*
>
> *I awoke the next morning to the feeling of my hand viciously scratching my legs. I had been bitten so severely that my legs had actually swollen. I counted over fifty bites on each limb. My experiment had not worked so well, and I spent the remainder of my time in the jungle covered in calamine lotion and mosquito spray! – CARYL*

FIRST AID

Before leaving on an extended trip, you are well advised to take a first-aid course of some kind. In most developing countries, qualified medical assistance is often far away. What you do on the spot could mean the difference between life and death, or at the very least, a slow or speedy recovery. Any time spent preparing for medical emergencies is never wasted, so always carry a well-stocked medical kit in your pack to deal with minor health concerns on the road.

Blisters

If a blister is not painful or inconvenient, it is best to leave it alone. It will eventually heal itself, reducing the possibility of secondary infection. If pain or discomfort make treatment necessary, do not pull the skin off the top of the blister. Push the fluid to one side and, while pressure is still applied, take a sterilized needle and gently pierce it horizontally into the bottom of the blister. The needle should be sterilized with alcohol, a lighted match or boiling water. This process may need to be repeated after ten or twelve hours. Keep the area dry and clean.

Breaks and Sprains

If you have the misfortune to sprain or break a limb while traveling, seek medical attention immediately. En route rest and elevate the injured limb. Cold applications of ice, snow or cold water will help reduce swelling and pain. Compression also adds comfort and helps reduce swelling.

Burns

If other treatments are not available, minor burns can be immediately flushed with cool water for ten minutes. This water wash will help keep the burn from spreading to other skin tissue while acting as a temporary pain-killer. Raising the burn above the level of the heart will also help ease the pain. Above all, never put butter or margarine on burns. They retain heat in the tissues, increase discomfort and provide an excellent breeding ground for infectious bacteria.

Do not break burn blisters. If they break accidentally, keep the area clean and covered with a sterile bandage. If pain is a problem, use two tablets of acetaminophen every four to six hours as needed.

Chapped Lips

If you suffer from chapped lips, don't lick them! It is one of the worst things you can do. When the moisture from licking your lips evaporates, so does the lips' natural moisture. In lieu of lip balm, try rubbing your finger on the side of your nose, picking up a little of the skin's natural oils.

Then rub this on your lips. This is the kind of moisture your lips are searching for in the first place. Remember to drink plenty of fluids and apply lip balm frequently.

Itching

For rectal itching caused by a yeast infection, try applying plain, unflavored yogurt. The good bacterial culture competes with the yeast. If you itch from humidity, friction or just too much wear and tear on the area, make an effort to keep it clean and dry. Expose the area (discreetly, of course) to as much fresh air and sunlight as possible.

Toothaches

Hot and cold water will aggravate sensitive teeth, but swishing with warm salt water (two to three tablespoons [25–45 mL] per glass) will relieve some pain. A saltwater rinse will clean the infected areas around the tooth and flush out any irritating pieces of debris. Another emergency measure, when no dentist is immediately available, is to rub a piece of ice on the V-shaped area between your thumb and forefinger for about five to seven minutes or until the area goes numb. Apparently, this is an effective general method of relieving pain. Clove oil and Ambesol are also good for on-the-spot pain treatment. Just daub a little on the affected area with your finger. Take acetaminophen or codeine in recommended doses every two to four hours if pain is severe.

HOSPITALS

Avoid stays in hospitals at all costs in developing countries. There is a distinct possibility of coming out with more problems than you had going in. If circumstances offer no other options, arrange to have a trusted companion tend to your needs for food, drink and hygiene because chances are good that the hospital won't.

TIPS FOR TRIPS

- If you are in a developing country and urgent medical attention is required, do not wait for an ambulance. In most developing countries, ambulances take a long time to arrive, if they ever do. You are better off being loaded into a vehicle and driven to the hospital. A North American or European physician would cringe at the thought, but sometimes there is no other option. You must, however, be very careful to have the nature of your injuries assessed and prevent movement or trauma in the affected area.

- If hospitalized, ensure you get a statement, itemizing all your expenses for doctor, room, medication and so forth. Complete documentation will be needed for insurance purposes.

- If you need an injection, make sure the nurse or doctor opens the disposable syringe package in front of you and watch them throw it away after. This is the best you can do to guarantee that a syringe from a package is safe. Remember, however, that people scour hospital garbage to locate used needles. Any that are found are washed, repackaged, then sold back to the hospital.

▣ If tests require a sample of stool or urine, make sure the container has been sterilized to facilitate accurate results.

Slow night in the snake oil business.

Mental Health

Mental health is probably the most important factor influencing the success of your journey abroad. The way you think and feel will affect all aspects of your trip, from your physical well being and resistance to disease to your relations with others.

CULTURE SHOCK

Culture shock is a reality that should not be underestimated. While personal temperament, experience and familiarity with your destination will affect the severity of culture shock, you should always expect to go through a period of adjustment. Though the full impact of culture shock takes time to strike home, the first pangs often appear the moment you leave customs and enter the main airport terminal. Suddenly, you are confronted with the realization that you are on your own. Sure, there is an unending stream of taxi drivers, hotel reps and potential tour guides willing to bend over backward for your attention. But still, it is you, and you alone, who must sift through the barrage of stimuli and decide how to make it from the airport to your hotel with the least amount of hassle and expense.

As much as culture shock is influenced by a change in environment, it also is influenced by a change in routine. You are in an unfamiliar land, and after the initial excitement wears off, you encounter the impact of the obvious: You no longer drive to work but take public transport everywhere. You spend money instead of making it. You no longer dine on familiar food. You can no longer

81

watch TV when you are bored or head for a hot tub when you are stiff and stressed. This in itself is enough to provoke anxiety. It's little wonder that you may feel out of sorts.

Extended travel in unfamiliar environments, especially on a shoestring budget, will test both your physical, mental and sometimes spiritual health, and you must consciously prepare yourself to cope.

TIPS FOR TRIPS

- Fostering a positive attitude has a profound effect on your immune system, which is in turn reflected in your state of physical health. No matter how big your medical kit, a strong immune system is still your best defense against conditions of poor sanitation and hygiene.

- Keep some routines from your daily life back home, especially any physical exercise program. Though you will probably be doing a lot of walking through your day, sometimes this is just not enough to purge accumulated stress. Tai Chi, yoga, jogging and swimming are only a few of the many choices available. Meditation also is helpful in fostering a healthy state of mind.

- After a while, hanging around discussing diarrhea, cheap hotels and outrageous encounters with other travelers can get a little monotonous. Pursue interests like photography or sports, or the appreciation of architecture, history or art to provide purpose and direction in your day.

ATTITUDE

Travel is fatal to prejudice, bigotry and narrow-mindedness.
– MARK TWAIN

What is right, normal or acceptable is greatly influenced by where you stand at any given moment. With movement, many rules are subject to change. This means that you must always be aware of just what is considered proper when relating to local cultures. You are more than a guest in their country—you are a representative of your own!

In the heyday of the British Empire, Englishmen maintained that all foreigners understood English if you shouted loud enough. It may have seemed that way, but it was probably not the language that the locals were responding to but the force and arrogance with which it was delivered. This attitude may have served a British Raj in colonial India or a white plantation owner in Kenya many years ago, but it does little for cultural cohesion in today's world. Attitudes like these drive a wedge between the traveler and any honest, intimate level of contact with locals and their culture.

Travel Arrogance

Many shoestring travelers complain about how high-dollar tourism is destroying beautiful and untouched paradises. They are of the opinion that money alone strips a location of its natural beauty and cultural innocence. But budget travelers who happen to discover and lay claim to an unspoiled area do their share of influencing and exploiting the indigenous population and location. They too represent a measure of western decadence. If *Rambo* movies, Madonna's music and the average shoestring traveler are the sole points of reference in defining lifestyles of the West, then it is easy to see how locals' impressions become distorted.

In Malaysia the police had such a problem keeping undesirable travelers from sleeping on beaches or becoming poor examples for Malay youth that the government instituted a policy of deporting anyone displaying immoral or improper behavior. Those suspected of such activities and who could not produce what the Malaysian government believed to be adequate funds for the duration of their stay had twenty-four hours to leave the country—with S.H.I.T. (Suspected Hippie In Transit!) stamped in their passport. – WAYNE

83

Eco-Friendly Travel

The despoilation of local ecologies is often the most immediate and obvious indication of the effects of tourism. One only has to look at the naked mountainsides in Nepal to see that the wood required to cook meals for increasing numbers of trekkers has dramatically changed the fragile ecosystem. A rare black coral is no longer solely admired underwater but is now common merchandise in black markets the world over. Buses stop for a washroom break, then continue down the road, leaving a trail of toilet paper as a remembrance of those who have passed that way. No longer do tribes dance only for religious, social and ritual purposes. They now organize themselves to display and sell their ideology and trinkets to tourists. Your desire to encounter local cultures and have authentic experiences while traveling is understandable, but what are the costs?

Desires must be balanced by the need to tred lightly and leave no footprints behind. It is not necessary to buy an article of religious significance just to hang it on a wall at home as a trophy of your time away. If locals recognize that you are more interested in them as a people than in purchasing their way of life as a souvenir, then things may be different. You may find a way into the heart, history and mysteries of the culture you are visiting, and you may discover that memories are easier to carry than booty.

You may not be able to leave a culture untouched, but there are things you can do to reduce your impact.

TIPS FOR TRIPS

- Visit only protected natural areas.
- Participate in foreign cultures rather than visiting only tourist spots that cater to western tastes.
- Get involved in local customs rather than imposing yours on locals.

- Try to learn some of the local language. You will be amazed at people's response when they find that you respect their culture enough to carry on even the most simple conversation. If you are spending a great deal of time in one locale, you may want to enroll in a basic conversation course.

- Don't go looking for controversy. Talking politics, economics and civil rights (among other topics) is an invitation to trouble. If you get into a discussion, enter it with an open mind and proceed with discretion. Keep in mind that the locals are not travelers like you and may have different reasons for doing or believing things.

- Enjoy local cooking instead of demanding western food.

- Refuse to buy sacred trinkets.

- Boycott coral and sea turtle products (including skin creams, jewelry and eggs), most reptile skins (especially those from the Caribbean, Egypt, China and Latin American countries), products made of anteater, ivory from elephants and marine animals (narwhals, walruses and whales), birds (live or stuffed), artwork using bird feathers or skin, and fur (especially those of endangered species and spotted cats, such as snow leopards or jaguars).

- Promote cultural and environmental conservation. Observe how tourism influences and affects the cultures and environments you pass through.

In Antigua, Guatemala, I found a small school where I could study Spanish. The teacher there connected me with a local family, and for an entire month, I lived, found friends, slept and ate in Guatemalan surroundings. It was a great way to immerse myself in the culture while learning a language. – CARYL

CULTURAL ETIQUETTE

Every land has its own rhythm and unless the traveler takes the time to learn that rhythm, he or she will remain an outsider there always. – JULIETTE DE BAIRCLI LEVY

As you travel, the proprieties of a culture will always be at play on a subtle or obvious level. For the most part, common courtesy and politeness will be enough to get you through. Still, there is always the possibility of unintentionally offending someone or demeaning yourself in the eyes of the locals. Often the smallest, most innocuous gesture in your culture can be highly offensive in another.

 Some locals understand the indiscretions travelers typically make and instruct them promptly about their mistakes. In most cases, though, you will need to catch and interpret the signals informing you that you have just crossed (or stomped all over!) a sensitive cultural line. This signal could be embarrassment in the group, a quizzical look or upturned eye, but no matter what, you will definitely sense a change in the atmosphere.

To avoid such situations try to observe people in their everyday interactions and notice how they handle themselves in relation to others and events. If you know you might be in situations where certain rules will need to be followed, inquire ahead of time and prepare accordingly. Read the local newspaper if you can and get a feel for what is happening in the country around you. It will aid in your attempt to understand the locals' point of view and opinions. Remember that unless you plan to immerse yourself in a culture over a long period, you will never truly understand all the nuances of communication that come with it. There will always be a certain lack of intimacy between the local population and foreign travelers and, therefore, not all the gestures that you've observed can be imitated with equal results. Committing a few *faux pas* along the way will not result in the end of the world. It may even make for some very interesting stories once all is said and done. Remembering the things taught to you as a child about respect and manners and about treating others as you would have them treat you will help to keep social offenses to a minimum.

> *A group of travelers was spending a lively night of drinking and dancing in one of the few nightclubs on the small island of Key Caulker, in Belize, Central America. Sitting idly in the back, a few locals were occasionally stealing a glimpse at the TV in front of the dance floor. They seemed impervious to the distraction of flashing lights, gyrating bodies and pounding reggae. The evening was in full swing when I noticed that no one was watching the TV, so I reached up and turned it off. In the blink of an eye, a man from the back got up, worked his way through the crowd and turned it back on. He then informed me that this was the only TV that many people had access to, and after many years, they had learned to watch it through the noise, the distractions . . . and the tourists! – WAYNE*

While human communication is extraordinarily complex and governed by few universal rules, you should be aware of some general guidelines about body language, especially gestures involving your hands. Provocative hand gestures that you should avoid, unless you know otherwise, include pointing with your finger (your eyes or a nod of the head should suffice), thumbs up, the okay sign (forefinger connected to thumb in a circular pattern), the peace (or victory) sign, the raised, clenched fist, the hang ten (with a closed fist and the thumb and forefinger out) and the beckoning motion (using the forefinger curling toward the body).

There are probably as many meanings for a hand (and finger) gesture as there are cultures using them. Next to the face, the hands are the most commonly used body part in expressing oneself or communicating with others. Always try to be conscious of just what you are doing at any given moment.

Other body language to be conscious of involves body movement, posture and dress.

I was flying to Thailand, a country with a very conservative dress code, with a female companion wearing shorts and a tank top. As we deplaned in Bangkok, we were immediately stopped by a Thai Airlines official who requested that she change into something more appropriate before reaching customs and immigration. All my companion's clothing was in her pack, which was just then being unloaded from the aircraft. The attendant asked me to accompany her to the luggage while my companion waited in the arrival lounge. I removed a long cotton skirt and a blouse with short sleeves. With that attire my friend entered Thailand with no hassles. – WAYNE

TIPS FOR TRIPS

- First impressions make a difference, so try to keep your appearance presentable at all times. Locals are likely to size up their own people based on dress alone. Just because you are a foreigner does not mean you will be assessed and treated any differently.

- Avoid poor posture. Standing with your hands in your pockets and slouching against walls is disrespectful just about everywhere.

- Standing with your hands on your hips implies, almost universally, that you are angry and ready for a confrontation.

- In many old cultures the body is considered sacred with the upper half being held in highest regard. Touching someone on the head can be a sign of disrespect in some cultures. Taboos at the other extreme of your body include not exposing the soles of your feet to anyone, especially an elder. Likewise, refrain from sitting in a crossed-leg position with your feet pointing up toward another person's head. (If you like to cross your legs, it is best to cross them at the ankles.) Never point toward anyone or anything with your feet.

- Remove shoes and outdoor headwear before entering a religious building or, in many cases, someone's home. In some cultures, women are required to cover their heads when entering a temple or mosque. Above all, observe local practices and always dress appropriately, which normally means no bare shoulders, cutoffs, ragged or dirty clothes, exposed bellies and so forth.

- Always remove your sunglasses when talking to people or entering their homes.

- Nude sunbathing is generally disrespectful. Though it may be tolerated in some areas to please the tourists, it is usually frowned upon and should be done as discretely as possible.

- In some cultures, the right hand is reserved for all social contact while the left is reserved for body hygiene. Never eat, touch a person or present gifts with the left hand.

- Cover your mouth when you yawn or pick your teeth.

- Do not toss things to another person. Get up and place the object in the other person's hand.

- Calling your waiter with a gesture can be tricky, so be careful when imitating locals. Generally, a raised hand or the polite motion of writing a check should be universal enough to summon the waiter.

Tips for the Arab World

- Never stand or sit on someone's prayer rug. Prayer rugs are small Persian carpets (approximately 3x5' / 1x1.5 m). The border of the pattern pulls in close to the top, leaving space for boxes on each side where the hands are placed when praying.

- Public displays of affection are strictly forbidden, even if you are a foreigner and are married.

- Shaking hands is customary among men, with an embrace and a kiss on each cheek.

- Women should never be touched unless they raise their hand when introduced.

- Shaking hands with a child is looked upon as sign of respect toward the parents.

- Two male friends will commonly walk down the street holding hands.

- People traditionally stand very close to each other when conversing, so moving away may give the impression of aloofness. People of the opposite sex stand farther apart when communicating.

- When eating at someone's home, leave a little food on your plate to suggest abundance, which compliments your host.

Tips for Asia

- The traditional greeting involves a slightly bowed head and hands folded in prayer. The handshake is becoming much more acceptable, but avoid prolonged contact.

- Pushing or shoving in crowds may not necessarily be a sign of aggression. In most cases it is an acceptable means of getting where you want to go.

- Public displays of affection are frowned upon.

- Asian society regards personal control and restraint as a virtue, so becoming loud, angry, agitated or impatient is not viewed favorably.

- The feet–head rule is strictly observed in Asian culture.

- Holding hands is a sign of friendship between two men and is quite common.

- It is not unusual for a person to decline a gift up to three times before accepting.

- Clearing one's throat, blowing one's nose, spitting and passing gas are all considered acts of personal hygiene and are very common, especially in the morning!

- ◪ At the dinner table, let the host begin eating first.
- ◪ Refusing a certain food may be impolite. If you do not want to eat something, accept it, poke it around for a while and then move it to the edge of your plate.
- ◪ Silence during a meal or conversation is a sign of politeness and contemplation.
- ◪ Eating all the food on your plate implies that you are still hungry and want more. Try to leave a little food to suggest that you cannot eat another bite.

TIPS FOR INDIA

- ◪ The traditional Indian greeting is hands pressed together in front of your chest (as in prayer), a bowed head and the spoken word "Namasté," pronounced *na-MAS-tay*.
- ◪ Staring at the impoverished or physically handicapped is an act of disrespect causing humiliation.
- ◪ Always ask permission to smoke among others.
- ◪ Becoming angry and impatient will get you nowhere. You will only be ridiculed.
- ◪ Do not whistle in public.
- ◪ Refrain from touching people on the head.
- ◪ Pointing with the finger is a sign of inferiority. The chin is used to point and an open hand is used for directions.
- ◪ Shoes must be left outside when entering a religious shrine, temple or mosque. Women should cover their heads and are usually requested not to enter during menstruation.
- ◪ Wash your hands before and after a meal. When not offered utensils, use only the fingers of the right hand.
- ◪ If invited for a meal, try not to refuse food. If you suspect there will be a problem, let your host know ahead of time. Pressing your hands together, bowing your head and saying "Namasté" signifies you have had enough.

Many North Americans and Europeans are unfamiliar with the close-quarter conversations common to some cultures. These talks typically begin with a local moving

*closer to you than your comfort allows. You take a step
or two back, which spurs the local forward and closer
again in order to continue the conversation. You step
back once again, and the local moves forward. This
dance carries on until someone gives in or you literally
find yourself backed against a wall.* – WAYNE

TIPS FOR LATIN AMERICA

◪ Latin Americans stand very close and maintain eye contact while conversing.

◪ Handshakes are common as are embraces between close friends and relatives.
If one's hands are dirty it is common to offer a forearm to touch.

◪ Males should usually rise when women enter the room.

◪ A woman greeting a familiar man may bend forward and present her cheek to
receive a light kiss.

◪ Wait for everyone to be served before you begin eating.

◪ Try not to eat with your fingers (even chicken).

◪ Do not pour wine with the left hand and never hold the bottle by the neck.

◪ Placing knife and fork parallel across your plate signifies that you are done.

◪ Dress and act appropriately when visiting a church or religious shrine.

◪ Nude sunbathing is the height of disrespect.

◪ Place change directly in the hand and not on the counter.

*Eating "Completo"
Chile's National Dish
Best bring a snorkel . . .
It's a hotdog swamp of
mayonaise. mustard,
ketchup and hot relish.*

*Traveling across the South
American continent for the
first time, I often gave the okay
sign (with my thumb and forefinger) to indicate that a meal or
other service was acceptable. I
sensed from people's reactions that*

something was subtly wrong but never thought too much of it. Not until we got to Brazil, when I gave the sign again and a local friend quickly pulled my hand down. He explained that in many Spanish-speaking countries the signal (or a variation thereof) meant that I was gay and looking for a good time. In Brazil, it was an insult or an invitation to buzz off! Needless to say, that was the last time I used that gesture while away from home. – WAYNE

TIPS FOR AFRICA

- Because Africa is a continent with many cultures and tribes, it is therefore very difficult to give overall guidance regarding general social decorum. But follow the rules of common courtesy while you learn from the locals.

- A handshake is widely accepted when two males meet, but one must not shake the hand of a woman unless it is offered first.

- Try to avoid prolonged eye contact, which is looked upon as a sign of rudeness.

- Men and women generally maintain little public social contact.

- Dining is an important custom in many African cultures, so how people conduct themselves while eating says a lot about their character. To leave your good name intact, you should follow the lead of your hosts, be modest in your manners and how much you eat. Never refuse an offering. These small courtesies should be paired with common sense.

I had been invited to a small village in northern Kenya to celebrate Christmas day. In my honor they had slaughtered a goat, and it was hanging from its skinned legs with blood still dripping down its bug-infested body. As a vegetarian, I was not looking forward to the meal, but I smiled politely because I'd learned better than to refuse such a gift from my host. I swallowed each bite, thankful for the honor. – CARYL

BEGGARS

Begging is probably the world's third oldest profession (next to prostitution and sheepherding) and is not as easy an occupation as many would think. There is no shortage of people who truly need to live off the kindness of strangers in our affluent western culture. Mother Theresa once said that the world's most desperate and poor lived not in Calcutta but on the streets of New York! The issue is generally much more acute in third world countries, but wherever you are, the key is to recognize who is generally more deserving. Simply being young or having a conveniently crying baby are not definitions of genuine poverty, and there will always be those willing to con the naive and softhearted. When you give, ensure as far as you can that the receiver is truly in need, and try to appreciate the situations most beggars must endure. Truly unemcumbered giving provides an opportunity to reach across the barriers of culture and language with genuine concern for the human condition.

I was with a friend who was in India for the first time. I had to leave for a few moments and returned to find her surrounded by a gathering of street urchins and hustlers, a crowd that seemed to be growing by the minute. A man was cleaning her ear while she read his tourist testimonial book regarding the quality of his work. Another was braiding her hair, and a boy was

Street sleeper in Singapore.

attempting to shine her sandals. Others were selling her knickknacks, and still others who had no trade or talent were attempting to pass themselves off as masseuses, amateurishly massaging her ankles and legs. She had not invited any of them, but more impor-tantly she had not resisted their aggressive sales pitch.

She took it all in stride, letting them continue but telling them she wasn't paying for anything. When we attempted to leave, the pressure was on to pay for their unsolicited services. It took considerable effort to extract ourselves from the scene when a firm refusal at the beginning would have prevented it altogether. It's a lesson every traveler needs to learn. – WAYNE

TIPS FOR TRIPS

- Many children will accost you on the street. Try not to give them sweets, pens, coin currency from your country and so on. Your giving only encourages their behavior. In this situation a card trick or a moment of your time is better than money.

- Keep a small amount of accessible change in your pocket. When you give, be quick and discreet so other beggars do not see the transaction and hound you for more.

- Learn to say no without feeling guilty.

- If you decide not to give and a beggar follows and harasses you, firmly request to be left alone. If harassment continues, treat it as a threat and take evasive action, such as slipping into a store or calling the police.

While waiting to leave India by bus, I started playing a winking game with the small daughter of one of the beggars milling about. Before boarding the bus, I kneeled down and offered my hand in a gesture of thanks. She was surprised but shook my hand. Then others held out their hands. I shook every hand offered, and boarded the bus. As I took my seat, the mother of the child stretched her hand up to my window. She wanted to give me a gift. It was the balloon she'd been trying to sell, but she did not want money. When we shook hands tears rolled down her face. I will never forget what I received by offering respect to one who rarely experiences it. – CARYL

BURNOUT

"It's simple. Either you get the wave or it gets you!"
– OLD SURFING EXPRESSION

People have a way of saying they *did* such and such a country. On many occasions, they should be saying that the country *did* them. There is no doubt about it. Movement through developing countries is an exhilarating experience. It can be exciting, relaxing, intimidating, stimulating, frustrating and lonely. This is what travel through the unknown is all about!

It's inevitable that you will go through periods of depression and anxiety, including culture shock in the beginning, homesickness later on, and along the way bouts of just being plain fed up with all the hassles and inconveniences of budget travel. When you begin to notice that you are becoming increasingly short-tempered, overwhelmed, uninterested in food or exercise, or just not having a good time, you're probably encountering travel burnout. When this happens it's time to break up your travel routine with activities that remind you of home.

TIPS FOR TRIPS

- ◪ If constant movement is getting you down, then knock it off! Head to a comfortable environment such as the coolness of the mountains or highlands or the relaxation of the beach. Once there, just lounge around, resting and recuperating.

- Read a good escape novel, catch up on some overdue letters or start writing the travel book you know you've got in you.

- If you're stuck in an urban situation, see a movie (with subtitles, if you like) or find somewhere to watch satellite TV.

- Call a family member or a friend back home.

- Treat yourself to a little luxury or excitement—drinks and dancing perhaps.

- Eat well and sleep a lot. Head to a good hotel for a few days and eat in upper-class restaurants. Sometimes just the cleanliness and air-conditioning are enough to change your attitude.

- If you can't afford a good hotel, put on your border clothes and hang around the lobby (or swimming pool) as if you belong there.

- Go to your embassy and hang around. Read magazines or the teletype news reports while talking with fellow countrymen engaged in everyday work situations instead of the wandering travel life. This is called diversion therapy.

- For those who are religiously inclined, places of worship have a tremendously soothing effect during hectic times or bouts of loneliness and depression.

- Write in your travel journal and you may just find that you write your mood away.

■ If you have simply reached your tolerance level, leave. Even if you are sched-uled to be there longer, scrap your timetable and make new reservations to get out. Hanging around for no good reason wreaks havoc on your state of mind.

These are only a few suggestions. Do whatever you can to get back into a healthy frame of mind. If nothing works, it is time to consider going home. But most of all remember that a measure of boredom or depression after weeks or months on the road is natural.

Women Traveling Alone

Until recently a woman planning to travel alone had only a small selection of books to choose from on the subject, and none even briefly touched on the subject of harassment, sexism or rape. In the past there was little demand for this literature because very few women traveled alone. They traveled in the company of men. Today, western women are independent, have access to resources and are finally able to follow their dreams, one of which is seeing the world.

But this new-found freedom for women is not encouraged or even understood worldwide. Men in many foreign countries believe there are three types of women: virgins, wives and whores. Virgins live with their parents. No father would dare let his daughter travel alone unless she was worthless and didn't deserve respect. Wives live with their husbands and are kept at home. Whores live with anyone, anywhere.

Many situations a woman will encounter when traveling alone need to be dealt with differently than if she were a man or woman accompanied by a man. As a woman traveling alone, you will be watched and your behavior carefully observed. Men will look for clues signaling your purpose, your status and your worth. You must be able to demonstrate with subtle gestures and conduct that you deserve respect and must be treated with honor at all times. Walk with confidence, carry yourself with an air of determination and certainty, and act in a manner worthy of respect. This will make it much easier to deal with unwanted hassles from foreign men.

The view that western women are loose and an easy target is still alive and well in many countries. If you dine out and drink alcohol, smoke and share time with men, laugh aloud and tell stories, all without restraint, your actions can be interpreted in some countries as the behavior of a prostitute. What is normal behavior for you can be perceived as an invitation to be pinched, grabbed and groped.

Observing the nonverbal cues between men and women in foreign cultures is difficult, but if you can identify the invisible lines and act within the boundaries, your travels will be much easier.

In Morocco I couldn't become comfortable with the whistling, cat calls and hissing by men trying to get my attention. Everytime I passed a café the whole routine started again. For once I was going to try to change the outcome of the situation. One day in frustration, I turned quickly and sat down beside a group of catcallers. I asked if they wanted to talk to me or ask me something. They were so shocked at the confrontation that they didn't say a word. I firmly explained that if they wanted to talk to a foreign woman, a polite introduction would work better. They started to shuffle their feet and cowered in their embarrassment. I said my good-byes and left. I don't know if my actions made any long-term difference in their lives, but it sure felt good to say what was on my mind. – CARYL

WOMEN IN A MAN'S WORLD

In the patriarchal world of many developing countries, women are not in the spotlight but rather are kept in the background. Women have domestic roles while men take care of business. One of the first things you will notice as a woman traveling alone is the stark contrast between the number of men you encounter in your everyday routine and the number of women you don't. The marketplace and café are male domains, and most local women are neither welcomed nor permitted to participate. You may find that you are actually considered an "honorary man."

A further barrier to meeting foreign women is their limited access to formal education. Even if it were common to meet them in the markets or cafés, they may not be able to speak one of the western world's major languages. Even if they had the opportunity and means, foreign women may not want to meet you for the same reasons the men want to. If they regard western women poorly, then any association they have with you may tarnish their reputations. If they regard you with more respect, they may even pity you for not having a husband and a baby.

MEETING MEN

Some men may be persistent, overly inquisitive and perhaps even irritating. But try not to generalize. Others may be friendly and genuinely helpful. To them a foreign woman is a picture of the unobtainable, the mysterious and the desirable, all suddenly within reach. Some men may see you as a lifestyle enhancement opportunity. If they play their cards right, they can marry and emigrate to a country where a prosperous life seems guaranteed (or so they think). Be wary of premature declarations of everlasting love. If you do fall in love while traveling, don't let the moment take you too far. Romance on the road can be terribly intense, incredibly passionate and a fairy tale beyond your wildest dreams, but keep your heart in check. Once home, you'll find the realities of everyday life will start sinking in, clearing your head and taming your emotions.

You will perhaps even encounter local men who act as gigolos searching for the woman traveler who wants a special holiday romance. They will pursue you until you make it clear that either you want it or you don't. Like too many men the world over, they may translate the word *no* as *maybe, perhaps later* or *ask me again in another way*. Rejecting persistent advances may require all your communication skills, both verbal and nonverbal.

It is a mistake not to be cautious, but it is also a mistake to put all men in the same category. Some may be genuinely friendly. They may be interested in you as a person and just want to interact with a foreigner. If you do meet a man and would like to enjoy some wild nights, take the proper precautions and more. Until you are certain he can be trusted completely, don't let him take you anywhere remote or isolated. Also don't expect him to be up front about his sexual history and past experiences; in some countries, men do not talk about such things with women. In some places men consider wearing a condom unnecessary, uncool and unmanly. If he doesn't wear a condom, don't wait around until morning to leave. Chances are he hasn't used one with anybody else.

Be aware that in some countries casual sex is purely a physical act while in others it's a serious action leading to marriage. Know what the attitudes are before you indulge.

TIPS FOR TRIPS

- Learn the sexual attitudes of the country where you're traveling so you are better prepared for the behaviors you will encounter.

- Do not flirt or invite intimacy unless you are serious about it.

- Recognize that you may be conveying messages you aren't aware of. For example, maintaining direct eye contact could be misconstrued as a come-on.

- Be aware of a country's dress codes, and dress in a respectful and conservative manner.

- To avert unwanted lines of questioning or attempts to pick you up, travel with an invented, imaginary husband who always seems to get sick whenever you travel and unfortunately has to stay in the hotel room for the day. This explanation seems to suffice and lets potential admirers know you are not available or interested.

- If harassed, attempt to change the sexual dynamics of the situation by saying, "What would your mother say if she saw you acting like this?" Ask to see pictures of his wife, his children, his family. In many third world cultures respect for the family is so ingrained that thoughts of tarnishing the family's reputation will tend to keep amorous advances in check.

- If you are repeatedly bothered or even threatened, appeal to local women for assistance. Whatever the language barrier, they will probably understand.

Rape

It can happen. If you are ever unfortunate enough to find yourself facing this horrible predicament, remember that there are some things you can do to protect yourself. Most of all, take comfort in knowing that no matter what, you are not to blame. You did not ask for it, and you certainly did not deserve it. Being raped or attacked is an infringement of your rights anywhere in the world. It has nothing to do with who you are or what you have done. It is repugnant, it is reprehensible and it is a horrific violation. Be strong, be sure of yourself and be ready for anything at all times.

Tips for Trips

- Never let strange men know where you are staying, and do not be too quick to accept offers of accomodation, especially in countries where women traveling alone are considered promiscuous.

- Have your key ready before you reach your hotel room so no time is wasted.

- In unsure circumstances, walk tall, look straight ahead and move at a steady pace with a sense of purpose.

- Instead of walking, use cabs at night, and try not to travel alone. If you must travel at night, sit in the back seat directly behind the driver.

- If you are followed, go into the nearest shop and ask for assistance. Somebody intervening on your behalf in the local language will help tremendously.

- Verbal confrontation in public can be very embarrassing for foreign men, especially if it is coming from a woman. If you ever need to defend yourself, the first method is to create a loud and obnoxious scene. This will usually catch the aggressor off guard, forcing him into at least a momentary retreat and perhaps to abandon his intentions. If not, then it may serve to arouse the attention of bystanders who can help.

- Wear a whistle around your neck at night and don't feel awkward about using it.

- The less you carry with you, the easier it will be to run.

- In any perilous situation, yelling "Fire!" (in the local language) will solicit a quicker response than "Help!"

- If you are being accosted but the possibility of escape exists, yell obscenities as loudly as you can. They may bring attention and the possibility of help. They may fluster your assailant, and most importantly the act of shouting may increase the flow of adrenalin and thus your strength.

- Your best chances of coming out of a dangerous situation quickly and safely is during the first few moments. Try to change the dynamics of a manipulative encounter by communicating in no uncertain terms that you are going your own way and doing your own thing without a male's company or assistance. If this fails and the man becomes more aggressive, do whatever it takes to break his concentration enough to allow a surprise kick to his groin. You might, for example, act crazy or pretend to faint.

- If you are held from behind, stamp as hard as you can on your assailant's foot. This may shock him enough to let you go, and, if sufficiently hurt, he won't chase you.

- If you are being held down, don't waste your energy fighting back. Save your strength for an unguarded moment when you can strike at his groin, eyes or throat with all the power you can muster. Pull his hair, scratch, bite and be prepared to do whatever you can to get away because there are no rules of conduct applicable when your life is on the line!

- Never let yourself be taken somewhere else. You may be told that if you go with him you will not be hurt, but the chances are slim he's being honest with you. A relocation reduces his chances of getting caught while creating a better opportunity to do what he wants at his leisure.

- Give up anything if it means saving your life.

GYNECOLOGICAL PROBLEMS

Poor diet, resistance lowered through the use of antibiotics, tight clothing that doesn't allow your skin to breathe, lounging around in damp bathing suits and even contraceptive pills can lead to vaginal infections when traveling in hot climates. There are mainly two causes of vaginal problems: yeast infections, which are characterized by an itchy sensation, and bacterial infections, characterized by an unusual discharge or odor. Keeping the genital area clean and dry, and wearing skirts or loose-fitting trousers and cotton underwear will help prevent infections.

Yeast infections are characterized by an itch and sometimes discharge. Lowering your sugar and alcohol intake, taking acidophilus tablets or increasing the citrus in your diet can reduce your risk of getting a yeast infection by lowering your pH level. The common medical treatments for yeast infection are Monistat or Canesten vaginal creams and can be purchased over the counter. If you have a recurring problem with yeast infections, you may want to take a three-day treatment of the prescription along on your journey.

Trichomonas is a more serious bacterial infection. Symptoms are a frothy discharge and an abnormal odor or possibly a burning sensation when urinating. There may also be pain during sexual intercourse. An over-the-counter antibacterial vaginal cream called Flagyl is the prescribed drug for this ailment. If this does not work and the problem persits, see a doctor; you may need oral Flagyl. Male sexual partners must also be treated. If stricken with a case of trichomonas, soak panties in water for thirty minutes or so before washing with unscented detergent and rinse thoroughly. Wearing baggy clothing will prevent discomfort while on the mend. Moist, dark and warm areas are perfect breeding grounds for yeast and bacteria, so lounging in a wet bathing suit is a perfect environment for growth. Dry off quickly and change into loose cotton clothing.

To eliminate the risk of a urinary tract infection, follow the above advice and always ensure that you empty your bladder before and after any sexual encounter. Again, if these types of infections are common for you, it may be advisable to take a short course of treatment along in your medical kit.

If any vaginal problem does not resolve itself with cream or medication, or if there is persistant pain in the pelvis or even a fever, see a doctor immediately; you could have an STD like chlamydia or worse.

Don't be surprised if your menstrual cycle changes, becomes shortened or stops all together. It's usually only from the strain of travel or the change in routine and climate. You shouldn't worry too much about it.

If you are taking oral contraception and have a bout of diarrhea or vomitting, your pills may not be absorbed, so take extra precautions. Carry a copy of your birth control prescription in case you need to refill it overseas. The chances are good that they will not have your exact brand name, but there are probably many different types of contraceptive pills compatible with what you are using. Some birth control pills react badly with antibiotics, so talk to your doctor beforehand. Always carry condoms from your home country and keep them in a dry, safe place. If you don't use them, give them to another who will.

If you get pregnant while traveling, try to stay calm and clearheaded. If necessary, go somewhere else where you can relax and make a wise decision about what you will do. If you decide to have an abortion overseas, inquire about the laws and attitudes in the country regarding this procedure, but the chances are good that returning home will be your safest plan.

FINAL WORDS

As a solo woman traveler, you will face many challenges that will test your ability to cope, but meeting these challenges can result in a greater measure of self-confidence. That, coupled with knowledge and common sense, will assist you as you experience the world of overland travel.

Getting There

Your trip begins the moment you start planning, but it doesn't actually feel like it begins until you arrive at the airport, when all your plans, dreams and expectations run headlong into reality. With every step, you quickly and palpably realize you are heading away from the comforts of home, family and friends and toward—you're not sure. But ready or not, here you go!

PREPARING TO FLY

Making airline reservations is not the hard part. The tricky part is matching the times you want to travel with the most inexpensive fares. And using the services of a travel agent is no guarantee of getting accurate information. You may need to canvas the airlines yourself.

TIPS FOR TRIPS

- Request your seat assignment as early as possible to ensure the most comfortable flight.

- Kosher and vegetarian meals must be arranged ahead of time.

- Check your ticket for the correct number of coupons (pages).

- If you do not want to be bumped due to overbooking, make sure you arrive at the airport early for check-in.

- Identify your bags with a sturdy tag stating your name and address. Place a backup tag inside each piece of luggage.
- Remove any old destination tags.
- It is safe to assume that your bags will be mishandled, so pack accordingly.
- Secure or padlock all zippers and buckles on your bags to discourage theft.
- If accessories are attached to your bags, make sure they are well secured and have an additional tag affixed to them.
- If your bag is common or easily mistaken for someone else's, make it unique by adding colored tape, colored wool or a sewn-on patch.
- Call ahead to arrange for special or oversized luggage.
- Remove all markings from packaging for valuable electronic equipment such as computers and cameras. Label the packages as fragile.
- Ensure you have enough money for airport and departure taxes.
- Be aware of all currency regulations if traveling with large sums of cash or traveler's checks over us$10,000 (yeah, we wish).
- When arriving at an airport, read the departure monitor to determine your check-in counter and gate number.
- Never lose sight of your gear.
- Never carry other people's packages or let them use your extra luggage allowance.
- Listen to all announcements, no matter how monotonous or difficult they are to understand. One may apply to you or your flight.
- If you have a question or concern and there are long lineups at the appropriate counter, try calling the airline's toll-free number or main city office for assistance.
- Stay away from unaccompanied luggage. Notify the authorities or the airlines if any bag has been left alone for an unreasonable length of time.

Booking Your Seat

The seat assignment best suited to your needs can often make a long, tiring flight just a little more bearable. When you book and pay for your ticket, take the extra time to decide where you want to sit. The front of the aircraft is good for tight connections—you'll be last on, and first off.

The middle of the plane offers the smoothest ride, but you are usually over a wing, so scenery is limited. It's the best location in the event of terrorism because assaults begin at the front and back. The middle is also the most solid part of the plane because of the beefed-up support for the wings.

The rear of the aircraft provides convenient access to lavatories but is the roughest ride during turbulence. With some designs, the back also suffers the highest volume of engine noise.

If you need additional leg room, ask for a seat in an emergency exit row, but remember the seat comes with added responsibility if an emergency occurs. The seats in front of the emergency row may not recline so try to avoid them.

A seat behind the bulkhead usually provides extra leg room, but there is no place to store carry-on luggage at your feet, and you end up staring at a wall for the duration of your flight. It also makes movie watching difficult. A seat immediately in front of the bulkhead will not recline, but the one in front of it will, making long flights uncomfortable.

Finally, consider what seat in a row will provide the greatest comfort. An aisle seat offers more accessibility to washrooms and overhead storage, but napping can be difficult because of the commotion around you. The window seat offers privacy, the best view and the best napping, but it can leave you feeling cramped. The middle seat—well, somebody has to sit there. If you are traveling with a companion on a plane with rows of three, book the aisle and window seat. Chances are the airline will not find someone to sit between you. Even if they do, you can arrange a switch after takeoff.

CHECKING IN

TIPS FOR TRIPS

- Carry all necessary documentation (passport, visas, boarding pass, exit card, if required, money and proof of payment for airport tax) securely on your person.

- If your flight is delayed, remember to change all connections.

- Check luggage tags to make sure your baggage is going to the proper destination, and check that all straps and handles are secured so they will not be snagged on airport equipment.

- Always keep your baggage claim check.

- If you are delayed through the fault of the airline, ask for compensation (accommodation, food, free tickets or money). Agents have the authority to use their judgment in such circumstances. Check all conditions before accepting a free ticket as compensation for being bumped from an overbooked flight. Many times there are restrictions, and reserved seating is difficult, possibly requiring you to fly standby.

- If you decide to fly earlier than your scheduled flight without a reservation or standby, remember that you will be classified as a no-show on your original flight and will subsequently have all your future reservations canceled. Reconfirm future flights before or upon arrival at your new destination.

AFTER CHECKING IN

TIPS FOR TRIPS

- Find the gate so you know where it is. Do not wander too far and stay in tune with the movement of people around boarding time. You do not want to miss a flight because you were engrossed in conversation while boarding was in progress. Believe me, it happens!

- Watch your valuables when passing through metal detectors.

- Interdenominational chapels are available in most airports for those wishing to worship or spend some quiet time.

STRANDED IN THE AIRPORT

At some point you will inevitably spend time waiting at an airport. You can do several things to reduce the tedium.

TIPS FOR TRIPS

◪ Stow the bulk of your gear in a locker or baggage storage. Keep only your carry-on bag with necessities so you have better ability to move around unhindered.

◪ Keep necessary toiletries, a novel and a small game in your carry-on bag.

◪ Catch up on correspondence to friends and family and entries in your journal.

◪ Sometimes airports have a quiet area where you can try to sleep, but lights and air conditioning can be a problem. A blanket and dark eye covers will come in handy. Again, be careful to keep all your valuables on your person.

◪ Ask at airport information about things to do nearby—movies, shopping, recreation facilities.

ON THE PLANE

Some people find long flights enjoyable. But let's face it—long flights can test many people's tolerance for frustration and their ability to relax. Nevertheless, there are some things you can do to make a long flight more enjoyable.

TIPS FOR TRIPS

◪ Clothing is important for comfort and safety. Dress in loose-fitting garments and wear comfortable shoes and consider packing slippers in your carry-on bag. You may want to pack a sweater, but remember it's easier to ask for a blanket than to peel off or put on layers of clothing.

◪ Carry an extra toothbrush and some toiletries in case your flight is delayed and your baggage has been loaded.

◪ If you have a cold, take a decongestant or nasal spray before boarding to reduce the severity of compression discomfort.

◪ If you are susceptible to airsickness take medication before departure.

- Chewing gum or candy, swallowing hard or yawning can all help relieve the discomfort of changes in cabin pressure.

- The air on planes during flights is very dry. Keep skin lotion handy.

- Wear regular eyeglasses rather than contact lenses, which may make your eyes dry and sore in the plane's artificial environment.

- Expect a lot of traffic if sitting next to the galley or washroom.

- If you are not happy with your seat location or need a place to lie down, go to the back of the plane. Airlines tend to stuff everyone up front.

- For sleeping, earplugs and eye covers or dark sunglasses are helpful. Walkmans (on or off) are good for ignoring boring or intrusive passengers.

- If you like to read from the selection of magazines on board, search them out immediately after locating your seat (but only if it doesn't cause too much commotion with other passengers getting to their seats). If you wait until attendants come to you, the selection may be greatly reduced.

- No matter how many flights you have been on and how many times you have heard the cabin attendants go through their safety routine, listen and remember. If you ever need to act in case of an emergency, you will be prepared. Know how many rows it is to the emergency exit.

- Attach the seat belt around your hips, not your stomach. It is important during turbulence to stay seated with your seat belt fastened.

- Be careful when opening the overhead flight bin during or at the end of your flight. Inflight motion may have caused bags to shift.

- Refrain from using computers or electronic devices, which may interfere with the aircraft's instruments. Ask if you are not sure.

- Long flights and long legs don't mix. Get used to it. In more cases than not, the bus seats in third world countries are worse! If there is a strain on your back, raise your knees higher than your hips for a short time. This position relieves some of the pressure.

- Don't become too friendly with an unaccompanied child. You might end up as a baby-sitter for the duration of the flight.

- Local people on your flight can be good sources of activities, restaurants and sight-seeing. Don't be afraid to ask.

Arrival

Arriving in a foreign country can be both exhilarating and terrifying. All your plans, all your research and all your preparations are about to be put to the test. As soon as your feet hit the tarmac or the train station platform, perhaps thousands of miles from home, the life you have lead until now may be changed forever by the experiences that await you.

WARNING OF IMMIGRATION

Malaysia welcomes bona fide tourists but not hippies! You are therefore advised to dress, behave and live decently in hotels as becoming a bona fide tourist. If you are found dressed in shabby, dirty or indecent clothes or living in temporary or makeshift shelters you will be deemed a hippie. Your visit pass will be canceled and you will be ordered to leave Malaysia within 24 hours.

Director of Immigration
MALAYSIA

Walking across the hot tarmac I momentarily bask in the transition zone separating the plane (all that we are accustomed to) and the terminal, gateway to the third world and the inevitable "come what may." These are our last few moments of anonymity before willingly stepping into the jaws of customs and immigration, where we are soon to be processed, passed through the terminal and then spit out into the local world of chaos, heat, taxi drivers, money changers, beggars and hotel hustlers. Let the games begin! – WAYNE

CUSTOMS AND IMMIGRATION

The exhilaration of arriving at your long-awaited destination may be quickly stifled by a bad experience at customs and immigration. Although the reasons for unpleasant encounters with government officials may sometimes seem arbitrary, generally you can make the procedure easier and faster by having all of your documents—visa, permits, vaccinations, onward travel plans—ready for inspec-

115

tion when you arrive. Being organized and prepared will make the jobs of customs officials easier. On the other hand, if you must scramble for a pen in your purse or papers in your pack, you are more likely to give officials a reason for detaining you.

TIPS FOR TRIPS

- Answer officials' questions, but never volunteer information. Keep your reason for visiting simple: Tourist!

- If asked to go into an interrogation room, request the presence of a friend or fellow traveler. This may not be feasible or even permissable, but you should err on the side of safety whenever possible.

- If confronted with a possible bribe situation, feign ignorance and stall by asking for explanations. Generally, officials will quickly tire and move you on.

- Always be polite and respectful no matter how irritated or frustrated you may be.

Land Border Crossings

There is always something exciting about crossing a land border. Perhaps it's that you're entering an unfamiliar country or just glad you're finally getting out of the country you were in. Perhaps it symbolizes another step forward or even something as small as a new addition to the passport stamp collection. Maybe it's the faint air of mystery and romance cultivated through paperback books and movies. Maybe it's just that a change is as good as a rest.

New beginnings, new money, new language, new sites, new attitude, new features, new scenery—whatever the reason, crossing a border by land is an unpredicatable affair. Sometimes it can be very organized and simple. You get processed by both countries quickly and are on your way. Other times it's a nightmare involving diplomatic problems, bureaucratic red tape, transport strikes, holidays, extortion and more. Crossing a border can take hours or days that may even stretch into weeks. Sometimes you can wait it out. Other times you will have to go to another crossing, or worse, change your travel plans altogether.

Arrive at the border prepared for whatever possibilities may arise. You should try to make yourself as presentable as possible. All your papers—visa, permits, taxes, vaccinations—should be in order. Be prepared to declare that you have enough funds to support yourself for much longer than you expect to stay. In some cases, depending on the country, have some small bills in your pockets or easily accessible in case a little *baksheesh* ("bribe") is expected by the officials.

On the overland trail, my limited daily wardrobe consisted of clothing purchased en route and a few comfortable and very worn shirts, pants, dresses and shorts from home. I looked like any other seasoned budget traveler, but when I came to a border or was conducting official business, I drastically changed my outfit and outward appearance. I chose a clean shirt, tucked it in and buttoned it all the way up. I combed my hair neatly. I always knew that official interactions would be easier for me if I looked presentable and respectable.– CARYL

Artist's impressions are subjective, and border officialdom often takes a narrow view of what art is beneficial to their nation's interest. A sketchpad is slipped down the front of the artist's pants.

Having everything in order is no guarantee that you will be allowed to enter a country. At the border there are no rules except those set by the border guards. They may turn you away simply because they do not like your looks although this seldom happens. If there is a problem it can usually be worked out with patience, diplomacy and a little smooth talking.

*I had been on the bus for over thirty hours sitting
beside a smelly, dirty and disheveled-looking traveler.
As we approached the border of Malaysia he finally
decided to start talking to me. We got off the bus, and
all of a sudden I was his best friend. I didn't want to
talk to him, nor did I want to be seen with what officials would consider a hippie.*

*I stood in line waiting to go through immigration,
hoping that the suspicious traveler would not stand
near me. He did. As we got to the front of the line, I
could tell he was nervous. Suddenly, he turned and
started to run away from the border. We were all
shocked. Officials caught him quickly.*

*As he walked past me with his hands cuffed behind
his back, he shrugged as if to say, "I tried and I failed."
I don't know what he was caught for or what he had
done. All I knew was that my instincts were right. I
was glad I had not befriended him because I too may
have been taken away simply because he pretended to
know me.* – CARYL

TIPS FOR TRIPS

- Know the maximum amount of time granted for a stay in your destination country and ask for it. Inspect your entry stamp closely to make sure that everything
  is in order and that you have been granted the amount of time requested.

- In some countries you may not want to declare all your money if you wish to
  take advantage of the country's black market. However, many times govern-
  ments demand currency conversion receipts when you are leaving the country.
  If your financial reserves do not balance with your exchange certificates, compensation or a fine must be paid.

- Find a secure spot and stash a little cash. If you are searched for any reason and
  the money is found, feign ignorance. Tell officials it was saved only for an emergency and is never counted as travel funds. With a little friendly persuasion officials may allow you to declare a sum of your choosing.

▱ Many immigration cards ask for a local address. Give the name of a moderately priced but respectable hotel or the American Express office. If you are required to present an itinerary, be vague and ask if you will be held to it.

▱ Make photocopies of all permits you may require and, if asked, surrender only the copies, not the originals.

▱ When traveling between countries with a history of mutual hostility, you may not want proof of travel through such controversial territory. You may need to request that your visa and all subsequent stamps be placed on a separate piece of paper so they are not permanently fixed in your passport for all to see. Even if such a request is approved, never assume it will be honored at the moment of truth. Once your passport has been stamped there is no turning back unless you want to get a new passport. Watch the official closely and be sure to have a piece of paper handy to receive the stamp.

GOVERNMENTS, OFFICIALS AND CLERKS

Dealing with government officials and clerks, especially in third world countries, deserves special attention because they often have the power to help or hinder you. Start with the attitude that even if they do not appear to be as efficient and organized as their counterparts back home, they are still people trying to do the best job they can. Inevitable delays or problems processing your requests are usually the fault of the system in which the officials work. If you expect their cooperation you should be willing to enter into any kind of dialogue with a healthy dose of respect. Be patient. Everything takes time, so being in a hurry is futile and will only deepen your dilemma. Plan for delays and waiting so you can spend your time doing constructive things instead of fuming at the bureaucracy and the inefficiency of it all.

Like anyone else, government officials don't want to have their time wasted, so get right to the point by requesting their assistance. Don't be condescending or arrogant, and do not expect them to jump at even the simplest request.

If your request is going to be delayed or denied, then you must start working on the personal factor. Talk to them. Create some kind of personal rapport by asking about family, country and pastimes, all of which are good icebreakers. Like anyone else, government officials want to feel that they are interesting and that their work is important and worthwhile. Appreciate their efforts and thank them for their help. If they truly cannot help you, then ask them to recommend someone who can without jeopardizing their sense of self-worth.

Black market currencies.

Undeclared 'hard' currencies (for black marketeering).

Extra passport with Israeli visa.

'Controversial' sketchpad.

Controversial guide-book saying unflattering things about the president.

Bear in mind that people may be willing to listen to you even though they cannot help you. Don't waste time on people who can only smile and nod their heads. If you think western bureacratic practices can be muddled and confusing, then expect what you're not familiar with to be even more so. Accept the local policy or practice because in most places all the explaining in the world won't cause them to deviate from what they are accustomed to.

No matter how frustrating a foreign bureacracy can be, don't lose your sense of humor. After the worst is over, an annoying experience can make for a very entertaining story. Try to see it in that light while it is happening. You will be amazed at how fast your blood pressure returns to normal.

BAGGAGE CLAIM

If your bags are lost or damaged, contact an airline official and deal with it on the spot. The airlines are responsible to you as a paying customer by the Warsaw Act (printed on the back of one of your ticket coupons). The airline must provide limited compensation on delayed, lost or damaged luggage. Before leaving the baggage claim area make sure the bag you have is your own. You would be surprised at how many look alike.

DEPARTING THE AIRPORT

Now that you have cleared customs and picked up your bags, you should reconfirm any ongoing flights. Then you want to get from the airport to a hotel with as little hassle and expense as possible. Before leaving the airport, which may be the last bastion of western logic and standards, you need to know where you are going and how to get there. At this point it is wise to consider convenience above expense.

If you haven't chosen a hotel from your travel guide or by talking to people on the plane, ask likely travelers at the baggage claim or main terminal. Check around the airport for people who appear to be traveling in the same manner and on the same budget as you and ask them for advice.

Once you have a hotel name, go to the information counter and ask for a map of the city (bilingual, if available). Get directions, find out the options for transport and ask for the approximate fares to your destination. Any worthy airport information facility should be experienced in fielding your questions. Ask if there is a prepaid taxi facility in the airport so you can arrange payment before even walking out of the terminal. This relieves you from a lot of guesswork and pressure. Bargaining is the last thing you want to deal with after a long flight.

Once you know where you're going, how you will get there and how much it will cost, you will need to change a little money into local currency. Change as little as possible because the exchange rate at most airports is usually less favorable than on the streets or in the banks. Convert just enough money to get you to your hotel and have a good meal, unless you are arriving outside of banking hours or on a statutory holiday.

If being frugal is important, you can shave costs even upon your arrival. Find a few other travelers heading to the same area of town and split the cost of a cab. Ask if there is a group taxi. Another option is to walk outside the airport gates and take a local taxi. They are guaranteed to be half the amount of any taxi within the airport facilities. Just make sure you don't compromise safety for price. Above all, ensure that your transportation *is* a *bona fide* taxi.

JET LAG

If jet lag is a serious concern, then skip the parties the night before your flight, drink a lot of water, avoid in-flight alcohol and make it a point to sit on the side of the plane exposed to sunlight. This way you can monitor when you want it to be day or night. A good workout at your destination will get your metabolism going and help you adjust more quickly and sleep more easily. Walking in the fresh air and strolling barefoot on cool grass works wonders. Researchers are currently developing a pill to facilitate quicker adjustment to time changes. For now, though, jet lag is just one of those travel inconveniences.

Jet lag affects those traveling from east to west more severely than those traveling in the opposite direction. For example, it will probably take twice as long for your biorhythms to adjust at your destination when flying from Hong Kong to Los Angeles than the other way.

Settling In

CHOOSING A HOTEL

When revisiting many budget hotels, I am amazed at their uncanny ability to maintain such a consistent state of decay. In days past, lack of maintenance made their immediate future seem questionable, and I am astonished to find them still standing, let alone open for business. Everything looks the same: the dirt in the corners, cracked glass in the windows, curled wallpaper. The list goes on and on. It may never get any better, but incredibly enough, many don't seem to get any worse. They are frozen in time, as if the look of deterioration and neglect were an image they wanted to preserve. – WAYNE

Your flight may have been long and tiring, your movement through customs and immigration slow and complex, and your search for accomodation information difficult, but you must be diligent in selecting a hotel that is well located, safe and meets your budget. If you want to avoid the hassles of looking for lodging after a long flight, consider booking in advance for the night of your arrival. Topping the list of your concerns should be security (more important than price), location, toilet facilities, availability of hot water, comfort, cleanliness and room location (at the back of the hotel is usually best). Keep in mind that around the world conditions in budget hotels will range from ramshackle, bug-infested, security nightmares to humble, clean and warm. In most developing countries, travelers stay in hotels (even if they're not the Hilton) because they offer extremely low room rates, a variety of amenities and convenient location.

TIPS FOR TRIPS

- If a taxi driver attempts to recommend a hotel different from the one you've selected, take his advice with a grain of salt. He is probably getting a commission. Many times, though, a taxi driver is well enough informed to steer you in the right direction, even if he is acting in his own best interests. Make sure he is prepared to take you to your original choice for no extra charge if you do not like his selection.

- What's in a name? A lot in the lucrative accommodation industry. Be careful of deception. Many hotels have names similar to those that are more popular or recommended in guidebooks.

- Travel guides will inevitably lead people to the same spots (which can be good and bad).

- Consider a hotel's location in relation to facilities (shopping, embassies, transport, restaurants and so forth).

- Even if you find an inexpensive hotel in an affluent district, you will probably end up spending a lot to eat in the area.

- If you can't find a hotel, check airport, train or tourist information for a room-finding service or hit the telephones. Ask a cabby to go to another nearby town or ask a hotel manager for suggestions. If you are still unsuccessful, and you are with another person, consider finding a comfortable location for one person to wait with the bags while the other is free to move around the area in search of a room. If you are by yourself, store your bags at a hotel or at a luggage storage facility (bus or train station) and continue your search without them.

- Always try to arrive in the morning for optimum room selection.

- The lobby and the people hanging around speak volumes about the hotel itself. If you do not like what you see or feel, go elsewhere.

- Some places are like having a carnival outside your door. If you don't want excitement and all that comes with it, go somewhere else.

- Try not to be content with price alone. Many times, depending on where you are, spending just a little more money may result in much better facilities. Be flexible, and don't let your budget rule all your decisions.

- Check the room before accepting it. The hotel front desk will probably first show you the room that is hardest to rent. If you do not take it, they will show you a good one. If you are not totally satisfied, indicate you will go somewhere else or try to bargain for a fair price.

- Ask if the hotel has reduced rates for longer stays. If not, try to negotiate one.

- When staying in a youth hostel or a hotel with a curfew, find out when the doors are locked so you will not get stuck on the street late at night.

- Don't expect to find the perfect hotel at the perfect price on the first day. If you'll be in town for a few days, first find somewhere convenient. Then look around for a better price, facilities and location.

- Once settled in the hotel of your choice, do not call home from your room (if it has a phone); the surcharge may double the overseas call rate. Find a public phone instead.

I arrived in Santiago, Chile, late at night and went right to the hotel recommended by a fellow traveler. She said it was cheap but not cheerful.

I opened the door and turned on the light to a scatter of cockroaches retreating into cracks in the walls. A single light bulb hung from the ceiling, as did exposed wires. The bed had not been made and had clearly been slept in by a very "loving" couple. After pulling off all the sheets, I sat down on the lumpy army cot, which folded into itself with me in the middle. The floor would have been dirt had the leak in the wall not turned it into mud.

With no other options, I figured I could last until the morning. I covered the mattress with my plastic sheet, left the lights on and put on my sleeping shades. I was out the door at sunrise. The stay had cost me US$1.50, but checking into a new deluxe hotel for US$3.00 reinforced how a little more money can go a long way toward a more comfortable stay. – CARYL

Hotel Safety and Security

TIPS FOR TRIPS

- Hotels lose room keys all the time. At any moment there may be a hundred keys to your room sitting at the bottom of a backpack, in a collection jar or even down the road in the house of a local felon waiting to put it back into service. If the door can be padlocked and you can use your own lock, do so. You'll rest easier.

- Don't let anybody know your room number.

- If you are on a lower floor with windows accessible to the street, consider if there's a chance someone could enter or reach inside. Ideally, lower windows should have sturdy bars or grates.

- Be wary of holes in the walls. They have usually been put there by one of the local voyeurs. Catching an eye staring at you in a moment of exposure can be very unnerving.

- Check the stairs for escape routes in the event of fire.

- A room near the stairs or below the fifth floor provides a better opportunity for escape from fire.

- Most budget hotels don't have smoke detectors. If there is one, it will usually be hard-wired and not operational if the power goes out. It's imperative, therefore, to know where the fire exits are on your floor and to plan an escape route even if it's never used.

◪ If you're using a candle in a wood bungalow, make a base out of a tin can. Never melt it onto a wood frame, and always be aware of the possibility of fire.

In the Event of Fire

◪ Electricity is frequently turned off at night in some third world countries, leaving hallways dark and hard to negotiate. Memorize the directions, number of doorways and locations of handrails, familiarizing yourself with all escape routes and keeping in mind the possibility of bottlenecks being created by fleeing guests.

◪ Put your hotel room key where you can reach it when you get out of bed. If you smell smoke, grab your key, your money belt and your travel documents.

◪ If the doorknob is not hot, open the door a crack and peek out. If the hall is not too smoky, leave by the nearest fire exit. Close the room door behind you.

◪ If there is smoke but no fire, crawl to the exit with your eyes closed if necessary. Carry a wet washcloth in your pocket to cover your mouth and nose in case the smoke becomes too thick for you to breathe.

◪ Don't use the elevator—it's a deathtrap.

◪ Keep your key handy in case your escape is impeded and you need to return to your room.

◪ If escape through a fire exit is impossible and you must stay in your room, fill the bathtub with water, and soak towels and sheets. Stuff them around the door and any other openings to your room. If the bathroom has a vent, block it up with wet towels.

◪ Try to call the fire department or the police. If you speak the language, tell the police or fire department what room you are in. If you cannot reach the fire department, call the hotel front desk.

◪ Use a wet washcloth over your face to prevent smoke inhalation.

◪ As a general rule, keep your window closed unless breathing becomes difficult.

◪ Hang a sheet outside your window so fire fighters can locate you.

Hotel Bathrooms

Bathrooms in economy hotels and public facilities, especially in developing countries, often can test the limits of western travelers. Two of the most intimidating features of bathrooms can be cold-water showers and squat toilets.

A cold shower can bring welcome relief in hot, humid environments. However, in the mountains or during the winter months in some places, a cold shower is not inviting. If your hotel can't provide hot water, you have little choice but to grit your teeth and bear it . . . or stay dirty.

Indonesian 'Mandi'

TIPS FOR TRIPS

◪ At the risk of stating the obvious, the trick is to spend as little time as possible in the stream of cold water. Stand outside the flow of water and wet only your feet and ankles. Once they've gotten used to the temperature, move up your legs to just above the knees.

◪ Step back and put your hands and arms into the water.

◪ Once they are accustomed to the temperature, you can wet your head, but try not to let water trickle down your neck or back because these areas are most sensitive to the cold.

◪ Now you are ready to immerse the rest of your body. After a moment or two of this, it's time to expose your back and neck to the onslaught. It is still going to be a shock, but by then your body will be somewhat numb to the chilling effects.

◪ With your body now completely wet, step back, turn the water off for the moment and lather up. Rinse as quickly as possible, repeating the process if necessary.

Sound like a real ordeal? Well, it can be. In most developing countries you'll confront it on a pretty regular basis. Many times, no matter how much money you are willing to spend, hot water is just not available. Another popular form of washing in many countries is a bucket and reservoir of water. You do not get in the reservoir, using it as a bath, but rather stand beside it scooping water up and pouring it over yourself.

> *I arrived in Singapore after nine months of overland budget travel. Tired and ready for some pampering, I booked into a five star hotel. But regardless of how much I spent on accomodation, I realized just how completely accustomed to life on the road I'd become when I stepped in the shower wearing my rubber flip flops and hung my money belt from the curtain rod. –* CARYL

Travel liberates us of preconceptions about how the world should work, and this is never truer when confronting the matter of toilets. Toilets have different names in different places. They may be called WCs (water closets) bathrooms or washrooms, but it's best to learn the local term. This will save precious moments when nature calls and there is no time to play charades. Fairly affluent cities may offer western-style facilities. In other cases, toilets may look familiar, but you may not be able to flush your used toilet paper. The farther you venture from affluent urban centers, the more remote the chances are of finding a sit-down toilet. Often, the only facility available will be a ceramic fixture with a hole in the middle, accompanied by two footpads on either side. You simply stand on the pads, squat and eliminate directly into the hole. The body was designed to relieve itself in this fashion, so it is biologically more efficient. But from the point of view of comfort, it leaves something to be desired, especially for people who use toilet time for reading.

TIPS FOR TRIPS

- You will have to disrobe to some degree to give yourself enough flexibility to use a squat toilet. A good method is to lift one leg out of your pants or shorts and bundle them up to your thighs. Hold them firmly so they do not come in contact with the floor, which might be wet or contaminated.

- Most squat toilets will not accept toilet paper. If you cannot flush the paper, there will probably be a basket for disposal. Keep in mind that most locals do not use paper, so a trash bin is not always available, let alone toilet paper. If you don't want to be caught without, keep a supply in your pack. By this time, you may wonder, "If locals don't use toilet paper, what do they use?" Well, they use the age-old, tried-and-true left-hand method.

- If you find yourself needing to use the left-hand method, look for a source of water within reach of where you're squatting, either a reservoir with a bucket and plastic cup or a tap and cup. Both offer you a means of wiping yourself with your left hand (while still squatting). Pour water over your hand, down the hole, and repeat the process until the job is satisfactorily completed. Wash your hands with soap and water afterward. The left-hand method may be a bit disgusting at first and a little wet and uncomfortable for a while, but you can take comfort in the fact that if authentic experience in a foreign culture is what you came looking for, you've found one example of it.

  Since the left-hand method is standard practice for most people in rural areas of developing countries, you can understand why the use of this hand is highly restricted. Eating with or using the left hand to make intimate contact with people will bring an unfavorable reaction, as will offering the left hand for a handshake. In some countries the taboos are so strict about left-hand restrictions that the loss of this hand by accident or punishment can permanently banish the victim from the social eating table.

- When you are finished you will need to flush. This is achieved by using the bucket or cup to pour water repeatedly down the hole. Pouring the water from a high position produces quicker results.

HOSTELS AND OTHER ACCOMODATION

Hostels are an excellent alternative to expensive hotels, and they are a great place to meet other budget travelers, swap stories and hear about new places to visit. The price for a dorm bed (four to eight people in the room) is usually US$7–$15 a night with private rooms somewhat more expensive. On the downside, their quality may be unpredictable, they are often crowded, privacy is simply unrealistic and their location may be inconvenient. Hostels also set curfews that may restrict your activities to unreasonable hours, depending on the country you are visiting.

Despite potential drawbacks, hostels are the accomodation of choice for many budget-conscious travelers. For a reasonable fee you can expect shared facilities (sometimes including a kitchen), a common room, warm, simple meals and separate sleeping quarters for men and women.

If you want the price advantage of hostels but not the unpredictability of conditions, you may want to consider a membership in the International Youth Hostel Federation (IYHF). With over five thousand hostels in sixty countries worldwide, the federation is no longer the exclusive domain of the young (though the majority of guests will be between the ages of twenty and thirty). Most hostels have abolished age limits, and some now even cater to families. All youth hostels are run by a governing national body and are affiliated through the IYHF, which sets reasonably consistant standards of cleanliness, organization and price.

TIPS FOR TRIPS

◪ Hostel or dormitory life requires common sense and courtesy. Do not make noise or turn on lights while people are sleeping. Do not use or even touch other people's belongings without asking first, and try to keep your belongings neat and contained.

- You are sharing a room with unfamiliar people, so ensure you use the lockers provided to stow your pack. Lockers should be secured with your own padlock.

- Keep your money belt with you at all times (yes, even in the shower), and don't leave valuable items sitting about to tempt would-be thieves.

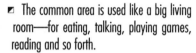

- The common area is used like a big living room—for eating, talking, playing games, reading and so forth.

- Some hostels offer TV and game rooms, but this is the exception rather than the rule.

- In the sleeping dorms, blankets and pillows are always provided.

- Some hostels do not allow sleeping bags, so check the rules when you arrive.

- Men and women usually must sleep in separate dorms, though some hostels provide co-ed rooms and many rent small double rooms or family rooms for a small additional fee.

- Always leave your travel clock alarm disengaged when not in use. There's nothing more annoying than someone's alarm going off when you do not have access to it.

- Use your own towel and sheet, if possible.

- Kitchens are usually well equipped with ovens, microwaves, refrigerators, condiments, dishes and cutlery.

- Label your food before putting it in the fridge or risk losing it to the free-food shelf.

- European hostels may provide breakfast rather than shared kitchen facilities.

- Hostels have no maid service, so you must clean up after yourself, especially in the kitchen, toilet and shower areas.

- Keep nonvaluable personal belongings on your bunk or in your locker.

- Some hostels may close for a few hours in the afternoon for general cleaning. You are, however, responsible for making your own bed and keeping your area tidy.

- Many hostels still have a curfew of midnight or 2:00 A.M. So you aren't unexpectedly locked out after a night on the town, confirm curfew time before leaving.

- ▱ With the introduction of smaller rooms (so you don't wake up the whole hostel) and combination doors (so night staff aren't required to monitor them), the pervasive curfew policy is beginning to fade.
- ▱ If you do stay out late, you will have to wake hostel staff. Bring a flashlight so you can easily find your bed and save yourself the possible embarrassment of crawling into bed with one of your new roommates.
- ▱ It's inevitable that at some point you will share a room with insects or rodents, so do not to leave food crumbs around to attract them. Edibles should be stored or hung up, and toiletries should be protected from contamination by a sturdy plastic bag.

Reservations for many hostels around the world can be made through your hosteling association via the International Booking Network. A US$5 booking fee applies, and you must pay for your accommodation at the time of booking. Reservations also can be made by calling the hostel directory or searching their website at: www.hostellingintl.ca

Most hostels are located in popular tourist areas. If traveling to remote locations, you may have to find a pension, bed and breakfast, guest house or private room. Staying in bed and breakfasts or local pensions can put you more immediately in touch with local customs and culture, but you will pay a small premium for the privacy and attention you receive.

Families throughout the world offer food and lodging at better rates than hotels, but for the price, you don't often get a tastefully furnished room in a cozy cottage with all the amenities. Many families simply want to supplement their meager income by renting a room. Quality will vary significantly, and depending on the country or neighborhood you're in, conditions may be squalid, so ensure you check the room before you pay.

Washing Clothes

Indian clothes washers are best described as those who break rocks with your shirt. – Mark Twain

As a budget overland traveler, your pack will probably contain only the clothes you absolutely need, requiring you to wash them on a regular basis. In all third world countries, reasonably priced laundry services are at your disposal. The price will depend on whether you want your clothes washed by hand or by machine, if available. Employing laundry services for the larger, more difficult items in your wardrobe is strongly recommended, but it's easier and more cost-effective to wash smaller things like socks and underwear yourself. Remember that water is a precious commodity in most countries and waste is not appreciated.

Detergent is cheap and plentiful, but time, energy and facilities may not be. If for whatever reason you must do your own laundry, learn the proper technique.

- Locate a sturdy plastic bucket large enough at the bottom to contain your foot.
- Separate the light and heavy clothing and wash only as much as you are comfortable with at one time. Heavy things may have to be washed by themselves.
- Soak articles in the soapy water. Step into the bucket, pressing hard to compress the clothes. Using the ball of your foot, continue to apply hard and fast pressure as you rotate the bucket.
- When you're satisfied that everything has been sufficiently pressed, lift items from the bucket, open them up

and return them while retaining as much of the water as possible.

- Repeat the process several times before beginning the rinse procedure. If the water is very dirty, you may need to wring the clothes out and repeat the wash procedure in clean water. Soaking newly purchased clothes in salt water will help prevent the colors from running.

- Wring out your clothes, having a friend help with the heavier items. Shake them out and rinse in clean water until no more suds are left.

- Getting all the soap out is very important. Be prepared to rinse several times.

There were no laundromats in Marrakesh, Morocco, so I decided to send my laundry out. When I picked it up later in the evening, not only was it not dry, but it smelled of gasoline. Back in my hotel room, I hung the wet clothes everywhere, hoping to air them out and dry them. In the morning the clothes were dry, but I had a major headache from the smell, and it stayed with my clothes until the next time they were washed. In this case it would have been far wiser (and a lot less smelly) to have done my own laundry. – CARYL

TIPS FOR TRIPS

- Be careful where you hang your clothes to dry in order to discourage theft. Ask hotel management about their policy on washing clothes. Many hotels will not allow you to wash apparel in the rooms.

- If you are in the bush in the rain and your clothes won't dry, share your sleeping bag with them overnight.

- It's always handy to have a rope and some clothespins.

- Gasoline works wonders on grease in clothing, and hair spray removes ink stains. Apply either to the soiled area and lather before washing.

◪ Separating the front of the garment from the back makes drying quicker.

◪ When using the services of a laundromat, make sure each article is marked with indelible ink or your name is sewn in a discreet place for identification. Show the laundry where your clothes are marked so they don't mark them again.

◪ If you want your clothes thoroughly dry when you pick them up, you must specify this to the laundromat when you drop them off.

◪ Make sure you have spare buttons if the originals are lost or broken, something that happens regularly when clothes are washed by hand on hard surfaces.

"Drop your pants here for fast service!"
– SIGN AT AN ASIAN LAUNDRY

CHECKING OUT

TIPS FOR TRIPS

◪ Make sure you check your room thoroughly. Look under beds, in drawers, on shelves, behind doors and even in the most unlikely place for misplaced articles. It's not unheard-of for hotel staff to hide guests' belongings and return for them later.

◪ It's usually a good idea to arrange transport to a plane, train or bus in advance so you can make a leisurely departure. Always budget extra time if your departure coincides with times of busy traffic.

◪ Review your hotel bill before checking out, making sure all charges are correct. Last-minute problems and delays can occur, so leave yourself extra time for the checkout process.

◪ If you want to share a ride when departing, check with other guests or post a notice on the hotel bulletin board, if available.

◪ Always be on good terms with the hotel staff. You never know when you may return.

On the Town

GOING OUT

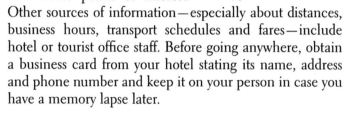

The traveler in a large unfamiliar city faces an immediate problem: how to get around inexpensively. The first order is to consult a map (bilingual if needed) or your travel guide and locate points of interest. Other sources of information — especially about distances, business hours, transport schedules and fares — include hotel or tourist office staff. Before going anywhere, obtain a business card from your hotel stating its name, address and phone number and keep it on your person in case you have a memory lapse later.

Late one night I shared a taxi from the airport to a hotel in Lima, Peru, with some people I met on the plane. The hotel was close to the airport, so the next morning I began my search for more centrally located accommodation, leaving my gear stored at the hotel. When it came time to retrieve my baggage, I realized that all I had to identify my lodgings was the name Hotel Welcome. Neither taxi drivers nor directory assistance had ever heard of the place. My only hope was to return to the airport and try to retrace my route from the night before. When I arrived at the airport taxi stand, I was surprised to find the same driver who had driven us the previous evening. Luckily, he remembered me and the hotel. – WAYNE

TIPS FOR TRIPS

◪ Before leaving your hotel, know your destination and how you will get there. If you're unsure, have hotel staff write down the name and address in the local language for you to show the cab or bus driver.

◪ When asking for directions, get a second opinion (and possibly a third). If you get a similar answer, chances are good the directions are correct.

◪ If you are attempting to learn some of the language, try to remember phrases that will help you get the directions you may need. The easiest questions can be answered with a word or two: How far is the market? The beach? The embassy? One block? . . . Two blocks? Is it on the right? . . . The left?

◪ Take note of telecommunication towers, tall buildings, major streets, large stores or prominent geological features that can act as points of reference.

◪ If you need to look at a map or even tie your shoelace, move away from the edge of the sidewalk so you are not bumped into traffic.

◪ Always walk with an air of confidence, even if you're unsure of where you are. The attitude you project is your first protection against being hassled.

◪ Crossing busy streets can be intimidating, so watch and wait with the locals. When they cross, stay close behind. Your experience with crossing traffic is no basis for staying safe in a foreign country, so stay alert at all times.

FOOD AND RESTAURANTS

Food is a sensitive issue with some people, especially those unwilling to experiment. Travel through third world countries offers unlimited opportunity to expand your tastes, and it's an experience no overland traveler should miss.

Food in developing countries can be an adventure, in both the best and worst sense. Time on the road reinforces the knowledge that we eat for two reasons: enjoyment and survival. In most cases it's a healthy combination, but there will be times when one or the other extreme will prevail.

You cannot, for instance, expect to arrive in a new environment, eat new food and sleep unusual hours (often in strange surroundings) without some effect on your physical well being. During the acclimatization phase of your journey, there are some special precautions regarding what and where you eat. After a few days you may simply take note of the eating habits of other travelers and adjust yours accordingly.

Tips for Trips

- Eat only fruit and vegetables that you peel yourself or that are washed with safe water. If you are uncertain, ask vendors if they use purified water.
- Wash your hands before eating.
- Avoid ice creams, custards, meringues, unbaked pastries and soft cheeses.
- Avoid unpasteurised milk products, including yogurt and milk that you suspect has not been properly chilled.
- Avoid food prepared with mayonnaise, sauce, cream or custard.
- Avoid open food displays such as buffets.
- Avoid undercooked foods, especially eggs, meat, poultry and seafood.
- Avoid raw, marinated or smoked fish. Ceviche (marinated raw fish) has been associated with cholera outbreaks in South America.
- Refrain from eating raw leafy vegetables such as lettuce or spinach unless they have been properly prepared.
- Avoid fresh fruits with broken skins. Watermelon and cantaloupe should be avoided. Sometimes impure water is injected into them to make them weigh more.

Once you've given yourself time to adapt to local conditions, you will inevitably find a wide variety of local foods that are not only edible but surprisingly good. Barring this, most shops and local markets carry at least some fruit, nuts, vegetables and baked goods, which can hold you over until you are more comfortable with the local fare.

Meat, poultry and fish are plentiful in most countries, but check the local sanitation conditions before partaking. Freshly caught ocean fish are usually fine, but shellfish, which may be harvested from polluted waters, may be suspect. One look at any butcher shop in most developing countries is usually enough to turn a person into a vegetarian, but beef, pork and poultry are generally safe in large cities where adequate cold-storage facilities are available. Alternately, if animals have been put to slaughter shortly before consumption and the meat has been cooked thoroughly, it should be safe.

All fruits and vegetables should be peeled or washed with purified water before eating. Dairy products are safe only if they are supplied by a reputable company and have been properly packed and stored. Be aware that when generators turn off at night, refrigeration is affected.

Do not be put off by unfamiliar foods. If it appears to be well cooked, and you see other people eating it, take a chance and try out a local delicacy. Food should be a major part of any authentic cultural adventure.

Tips for Trips

- Two good indicators of restaurants with healthy, palatable food are a clean, well-organized facility and staff, and a substantial number of local and foreign patrons.

- If you do not recognize anything on the menu, ask. If you cannot read the local menu, perhaps motion to your server that you'd like to see what's available in the kitchen. If the fare there looks good, point to it and smile.

- If you are with a crowd, order a variety of dishes to share so you can sample as many different foods as possible.

- The local people generally have no concept of what a good egg looks like after it's cooked. If you are fussy about the appearance of your eggs have them scrambled or boiled. (It's not uncommon to have eggs deep-fried until they are translucent, an unappetizing prospect for most westerners.)

◪ Soda water with a squeeze of lime or lemon is a good alternative to a soft drink.

◪ Yogurt, milk and sugar tame the bite of spicy foods.

◪ Food is naturally safer if well cooked, but overcooked food retains little or no nutritional value.

◪ Dining at open-air food stalls on busy streets isn't recommended because of the high level of pollution in many urban centers. Choose your vendor carefully, but by all means indulge if it seems appropriate. A busy vendor usually means your food will be freshly cooked.

◪ Salmonella is a real threat in some locations, so look out for foods that need refridgeration, like mayonnaise.

◪ If luggage space allows, consider bringing from home a small cache of packaged goodies for those times when the sheer novelty of foreign food becomes over-whelming and you're desperate for a reminder of home.

The brochette man. He's my kind of culture and the thing that keeps me going back on the road and off the couch at home. You can keep all the artifacts, the quaint travelogues, the textbooks and all the muse-ums. I take perverse pride in never going inside muse-ums to study local icons, but give me the popular icons like the street-corner brochette man selling kebabs of roasted meat done over an oil-drum fire. They were everywhere in Central Africa. One orders up the brochette, two or more per sandwich at 50 CFA each. To these on a french stick, halved, he adds a greasy curry sauce, sliced onions and perhaps (if I am feeling gluttonous and in good constitution) a peanut-oil fried omelette. The quality of meat can vary, but kebabs can be indescribably delicious. I am eternally curious and insatiable for these seeming trifles of street life that add up to create a culture. They are for me the reason to travel. Each to his own.
– Tony Jenkins, *Travellers Tales*

Nutrition

Travel necessarily puts your body under enormous strain. Though it may not always be practical, keeping a balanced diet is very important to maintaining good physical and emotional health. If, for whatever reason, your health begins to suffer, settle in one place and recuperate by establishing a balanced diet.

TIPS FOR TRIPS

- ▱ Eggs, tofu, beans and nuts are all safe sources of protein.

- ▱ Peeled or properly washed fruit and vegetables are excellent sources of vitamins.

- ▱ Grains such as bread and rice provide starch and fiber.

- ▱ If insufficient nutritional intake becomes a concern, vitamin and mineral supplements are always an option.

- ▱ In tropical climates, make a conscious effort to drink enough water. Do not rely on the cravings of thirst to establish frequency. If your lips start to chap or crack, your body is telling you it needs water. Irregular or dark yellow urine is also a sure sign of dehydration and the urgent need for more water.

- ▱ In humid environments, constant perspiration may cause salt depletion, so make an effort to keep your salt levels up by adding it to your food. In extreme, prolonged heat, you may consider salt tablets or electrolyte mixtures.

All vegetables in this establishment have been washed by water especially passed by the management."
– RESTAURANT SIGN IN SRI LANKA

SIGHT-SEEING

Budget overland travel is not restricted to the grassroots lifestyle of a foreign culture. Inevitably, you'll find yourself in locations rich in culture and antiquity, and that means, every so often, spending time rubbing elbows with the photo-snapping, safari-shorted, black-socks-in-their-sandals tourists doing what tourists do best: Seeing the sites!

When I returned home from one trip, a friend introduced me to his grandmother, who had been in the same area years ago. She asked if I had seen this or done that. A little embarrassed, I shook my head, leaving an unasked question: Why else would you go there if not to see and do all the tourist stuff?

Those were the days when I had more time and guts than money and curiosity about history and culture. Luckily, I've had the opportunity to return to many of those locations armed with a bit bigger budget and, just as importantly, a more inquisitive attitude. – WAYNE

TIPS FOR TRIPS

- Bring a flashlight to certain museums and historical sights. Lighting can be bad and display cases may be dirty.

- When viewing ancient temples, monuments or artworks, keep your hands off. The oils and acids from your skin are a potent corrosive. Over time they play a major role in the deterioration of these irreplaceable relics.

- Be careful when accepting handshakes or approaches from people around religious sites unless you are willing to make a donation to their cause.

- Find out the correct price for any tourist service and pay nothing more. If you are not given the correct price, try elsewhere. If you have no other choice, offer to pay only what is fair. Don't waste your time arguing. Pay and walk away.

- Avoid tour guides and taxi drivers who whisk you through the sites in order to get you into the shops, where they make a commission on what you buy. If you the guide is not giving you enough time to enjoy your sight-seeing, tell him to wait while you explore on your own for a while. If this doesn't work pay him what he deserves and send him on his way. You will be better off with an escort who is more interested in his professional responsibility than in being a salesman.

- Read about attractions before you visit so you are well informed about their function in the culture in the past and present.

PHOTOGRAPHY

An inexperienced photographer can take a bad picture with a good camera, but a great photographer can take a fabulous picture with practically anything! Many avid photographers travel with an array of expensive equipment. But remember, the more you carry the more you have to protect. A good single-lense reflex camera with a 28–120 zoom lens is usually sufficient, but even less expensive cameras take great shots these days. "Insure it and secure it" are the watch words when traveling with any camera, and it's not wise to travel with your equipment in an expensive brand-name bag.

Cameras can be terribly intrusive if the subjects have not consented to having their picture taken. Many cultures still see the camera as an object that steals the soul. They are understandably not too keen to have that happen. Be respectful of people, and do not photograph them if they have asked you not to.

In some cases, you may be asked for a small fee to take a picture of an interesting local. Some may use the money to purchase materials needed to perform a ritual to regain their lost soul but others just want to make money. So learn to distinguish between the two. One is a cultural nuance; the other is a business transaction.

I like to photograph people, and some locals have even asked to use my camera to photograph me. Giving my camera over (with caution) establishes trust and allows me to connect with locals who have never allowed themselves to be photographed before. When spending a day taking photographs, I carry small photos of myself to give those I photograph. I give them a picture of me, and I take one of them. Reciprocity is highly respected in many cultures around the world. – CARYL

Care of Cameras and Film

▪ Slides make a much more impressive showing back home, but tend to turn into a lengthy affair. Prints are so much more convenient in the long run!

▪ Avoid cameras that require lithium batteries. Though they may last longest, they are also very expensive and almost impossible to replace in developing countries. Always carry a supply of backup batteries.

▪ Dust, heat and moisture are very harmful to your camera. Take great care when bringing it to the beach or traveling through the desert. High humidity may promote the growth of fungus. Try keeping your camera in a plastic bag with a package of silica gel.

▪ Keep film as cool and dry as possible before and after exposure, and try to develop it as soon as possible. Many large urban centers have economical processing centers as good as you have at home.

▪ If at all possible, use film brought from home. Film bought in foreign countries may be old or have been exposed to sunlight.

▪ Store film with a speed of 400 ASA or higher in an X-ray–proof bag or ask security officials to manually inspect your camera bag.

▪ A polarizing filter helps reduce unwanted glare from the sun while protecting the lens from fingerprints and scratches.

▪ Carry lens cleaning tissue and a blower brush.

▪ If you have a new camera, shoot a roll or two of film before leaving. Familiarize yourself with its functions and versatility, and find out if everything works properly and the photo quality is acceptable.

▪ Your photographic record can become one of your most important vaulables, so pack it carefully and keep it secure.

Getting the Best Results

▪ Take the time to research the area you will be traveling through, and imagine some of the things you might want to photograph: people, culture, architecture, scenery. A little imagination beforehand increases your chance of recognizing a good shot when when you see it.

145

- If you find the right location but not the right subjects, be patient. Sometimes it is worth waiting to see who else will come along.

- If you are not in a rush, consider all the angles for best results. Where is the sun? What's in the background? Are there distracting shadows and surroundings? How will the same shot look if you wait a few minutes or walk back or forward a few steps? You can waste valuable film if you don't take time to think about all the angles for the best shot.

- If you are in a moving vehicle or if the subject material is moving, adjust your shutter speed accordingly. Fast shutter speeds are needed to freeze moving objects. If a blurred background is desirable, choose a slower shutter speed and pan the camera in pace with your subject.

- Natural light always provides a much more realistic atmosphere, but your flash can be handy in daylight photos to fill in unwanted shadows.

- Don't compose every shot horizontally. People and many other subjects lend themselves to vertical compositions.

- Always keep your camera secure but accessible for those split-second opportunities.

- The intense midday tropical sun tends to wash out color. Taking pictures at sunrise and sunset bathes the subject in a warm glow and gives an almost surrealistic effect.

- Look in all corners of the picture frame to see what's there and if there is a way to make it more interesting.

- Pictures of locals engaged in everyday activities are more interesting than simple portraits.

- Again, be patient. Sometimes it's the only way to get that treasured shot.

As a novice travel photographer, I was often self-conscious about openly taking pictures of strangers. In attempting to get only candid photos, I was always at the mercy of the subject noticing or moving before I could get things right. One day, while I was covertly attempting to photograph a group of women in ceremonial costumes, a woman off the tour bus walked right up to the group, showed them her camera and asked if she could take some pictures. They smiled, agreed and even posed, giving her the time and opportunity to get some great shots. I've since learned my lesson and now have a collection of many memorable photographs of willing subjects. – WAYNE

Camera Security

▱ Your camera may be worth at least a year's wages for many people in developing countries. Understandably, camera theft is a great temptation. Carry it in a nondescript case or out of sight in your day pack.

▱ If you want more security while carrying your camera, purchase a small chain from a hardware store and sew it directly onto the outside of your camera strap.

▱ It is always wise to consider security and cultural implications before taking a photo because many locations and situations are restricted. Especially, avoid the following: military personnel, compounds or installations; train and transport stations; bridges or border crossings; hydroelectricity projects; government buildings (including post offices, railway stations, satellite dishes, antennae); civil disturbances or coups; religious shrines, sites or rituals; and evidence of poverty, inefficiency or corruption. Any of these could result in the confiscation of your film and perhaps even your camera. If you are unsure about the acceptability of taking a photograph, ask, but be aware that if an official insists you purchase a "photograph permit," it may be a request for a bribe.

At a station stopover for the Trans Siberian express train from Bejing to Moscow, I decided to step outside for a bit of fresh air. The antique-looking trains immediately caught my attention, so I snapped a few casual shots. I was immediately taken by some officials to a private office, interrogated and told that what I had done was illegal. They accused me of working for another government and spying on them. Thankfully, after a lengthy discussion and the destruction of my film, they let me go. – YVETTE, UNITED STATES

PHOTOGRAPHY ETIQUETTE

In many developing countries, and especially those off the beaten tourist track, local people may not be familiar or comfortable with somebody taking their picture. They may feel it is an invasion of privacy or even that you are about to rob them of something very personal. Try to establish some kind of rapport with people you wish to photograph. Show your prospective subjects some other pictures that you have already taken of people, or let them hold your camera and look at you through the viewfinder. Do whatever it takes to give them a better understanding of what the camera is all about. If your subjects want you to send them a copy and you promise to comply, then do it! It's a simple matter of courtesy, and you are upholding the travelers' credibility for the next photographer.

Taking pictures with telephoto lenses or out of the windows of trains, buses or taxis might seem safe, but it still can be viewed as an act of disrespect. Keep this in mind while in situations where discretion is impossible. When in doubt always ask.

It was the day for the great Djenne market in Mali and the best opportunity to try to photograph people in their beautifully colored clothing. I sat unobtrusively outside for a few hours, quietly observing the women selling rice and grains. I watched as tourists quickly pulled out cameras and snapped shots of these women. The tourists would then wander back to their air-conditioned buses, to the outraged screams of women who were angered by this intrusion.

By midday, as the women watched me watching them, an unspoken dialogue began. They smiled and mimicked the actions of others, waiting for my response. I was soon invited over, and they joked with me in a language I didn't understand. They pointed to my camera, as if noticing that I hadn't taken a single picture. I handed over my camera and showed them the viewfinder. For the first time ever, they knew what was to be seen from within the camera.

Then, a dream became a reality. The women all wanted their photographs taken. They would stand proudly alone or with groups of friends. They posed, laughed and smiled, and I was soon out of film! I took down their names and addresses and promised to mail them the photos. Back in Canada, I mailed prints and a big thank-you note to each of them. The women of the Djenne market had given me a gift greater than just photographs. – CARYL

SHOPPING

Sight-seeing and recreation may be two of the biggest reasons people travel, but following close behind is shopping. Whether it is for souvenirs, presents, business or simple entertainment, somewhere along the way we will shop. But many travelers buy things they will never use and kick themselves for not buying what they should have.

When it comes to buying, a little forethought goes a long way in reducing the frustration associated with wasting money on ill-considered purchases, so it is wise to determine a budget for shopping. It is equally important to budget for the time involved. When planning your travel schedule and purchasing tickets, consider everything you hope to achieve in a particular location. With sight-seeing and routine errands, time can run out quickly, and shopping is usually the activity sacrificed. If possible, consult other travelers who have visited the same location about what they bought and how much they paid for it. The best shopping happens when you are relaxed and unhurried, especially when you are traveling on a budget. Savings to be had by shopping around will go a long way toward keeping you within your living allowance.

Tips for Trips

▰ Do not expose your wallet in the open market. Find a private location to remove a few bills for immediate purchases.

▰ You usually get what you pay for. If you are offered a deal too good to be true, chances are it is.

▰ Where you shop affects the price. Prices in expensive tourist areas will obviously be higher than in a local market.

▰ The more you know about product availability, the better you are able to decide what to buy and how much to pay. Shopping around also gives you a chance to become familiar with differences in quality and design. Murphy's Law states that when you buy something without doing your homework you always find it for a lower price and of better quality in the very next shop!

▰ Government-sponsored handicraft shops are a good place to get general ideas about what is available. Prices in these shops are typically top dollar, but the products are usually of the highest quality.

▰ Buying from the source of production does not guarantee a lower price. Sometimes urban centers have low overhead operations that provide lower prices and a better selection than those in more remote locations.

▰ If you are thinking about purchasing electronics or items that are readily available back home, consider the sale price of that same item and compare it to the cost and trouble of buying it abroad. Consider, too, electrical voltage differences between countries, and the issues of warranties and maintenance.

▰ *Caveat emptor.* ("Let the buyer beware.") Examine purchases carefully. If it is a brand name, make sure all parts are true and original. The lens caps on a telephoto lens may bear the name Nikon while the lens itself is labeled Nikkon. Always ask for a legible receipt in a language you understand. Also, be careful of bootlegged products. From shirts to watches to jewelry, there is no market untouched by "knock-offs." Even though you pay less than the original, be prepared to accept the consequences of low quality.

☐ Buying art or antiques requires that you do your homework. Have your purchase authenticated by an official receipt specifying the value and, if necessary, the age. The receipt should be written in your language and the local language to satisfy customs officials, both abroad and back home. Reproductions should be documented to avoid confusion or extra costs incurred at customs.

♪ CENT FRANCS LES MANGUES...
CENT FRANCS LES MANGUES.... ♪
CENT FRANCS LES MANGUES...
NCS LES MANGUES...

☐ In some countries it is illegal to purchase items with the intent of taking them out of the country. Religious and cultural artifacts are always questionable.

☐ Don't burden yourself with too many large or heavy purchases unless you plan to ship things home.

*Yaunde
CAMEROON*

☐ When browsing for promising locations, keep notes so you can find the shops later. Ask street or market vendors if they will be returning to the same spot, since it's not uncommon for street merchants to move from one location to another.

☐ Be careful when buying wooden products that may crack back home in an environment with different humidity.

☐ Practical souvenirs are better than useless mementos, which lose their appeal.

☐ A fair price for fair value makes you and the honest worker happy.

Bargaining

In most developing countries, everything is negotiable. Bargaining has been described variously as an art of social interaction, a science more calculating than chess, a sport mixing cunning with the thrill of the hunt and a game that, when done poorly, results in one winner and when done properly results in two.

Bargaining is a form of intellectual combat. In our travels we interact with foreign cultures on many different levels for many reasons, but bargaining is among the most animated, expressive and, in many cases, most satisfying of transactions.

Bargaining for the best price should be tempered with the philosophical goal of benefit to all. You can't expect to be treated fairly if you're not willing to reciprocate. With this attitude, bargaining can be an enjoyable experience, even entertaining, rather than a pain and an inconvenience. Attitude is everything when bargaining.

For some shoppers, every buying opportunity turns into a confrontation and an exercise in frustration. Thinking that all vendors are out to cheat them, they invariably miss the true benefits of the bargaining experience while reinforcing the traditional barriers between buyer and seller. They return to their hotels exhausted and ragged. Spending a day shopping with the wrong frame of mind is likely to wear down your stamina quickly, rob you of any kind of satisfaction and perhaps even increase the price of purchases.

With practice, patience and the proper attitude, you will become an effective negotiator and discover that bargaining is not about conning, tricking or manipulating. Bargaining is about the art of give and take. It's about compromise, honesty and persuasion. It's about respect for a merchant's time, circumstance and livelihood while expecting the same in return. It's about the impression you leave behind and the manner in which you relate to the merchant as a human being, not just a preconceived image or stereotype. You will

You've got to learn to negotiate!

always walk away with more than the object you have decided to buy or decline.

Tips for Trips

◪ Merchants are usually most motivated to sell at the beginning and the end of the day.

◪ Vendors can never lose. They know their costs and profit margins. The only difference a good bargainer can make is to persuade them to adjust their margins.

◪ Vendors are professionals who practice their trade every day. Don't expect to beat them at their own game. Strive to shift the advantage in your favor by making them want to sell to you more than you want to buy from them. They will then be more motivated to lower their price than you will be to raise yours.

◪ Do your homework. Think of who you want to buy for and roughly what you intend to spend. Talk to other travelers to see how much they paid, but don't rely exclusively on that price, since it's a reflection of their bargaining skill.

◪ Budget a day to window shop to methodically check prices and to establish benchmarks. Tell merchants you are only looking and let them do the rest. Once you have listened to an offer, smile and acknowledge it as if it were their only chance to catch your interest and walk away to something else or signal your intention to leave. Vendors may lower their price immediately to what may have taken long negotiation to achieve. Always thank them for their time, be polite and leave them wanting to see you again. When and if you do return, they will remember you in a favorable light and in the end may be more inclined to give you a better price than before. Continue the process of window shopping until you know where you are most likely to get what you want for the price you want.

◪ Never fall into the trap of volunteering what you believe is a fair price, even if it is ridiculously low. You will have lost your advantage because you are now trying to buy from vendors rather than having them sell to you.

◪ Never be drawn into bargaining as a result of boredom or merchant pressure. Many people are enticed into giving a price on something they were casually looking at out of a bored curiosity. They throw out a seemingly ridiculous price, expecting it to be turned down, and it is. They attempt to walk away only to have the vendor running after them. The merchant reminds them they have entered into a verbal contract, and in a way this is true. After all, they did offer a price. At this point, guilt may close the sale.

- Never be intimidated into buying. Salespeople reaching the point of losing a sale may resort to aggression in order to bully you into buying. They may accuse you of wasting their time or of not knowing true quality. They may even slander you. A common ploy is to follow you out of the shop and shout, "This is my last price. If you do not buy now, this price will not be honored if you come back." Of course, the price will be honored if you return because the motivation to make the sale is just as strong.

- Try not to counteroffer with a price so low that you not only insult the seller but also show your inexperience at bargaining.

- If you and a vendor have become genuinely confrontational and are losing respect for each other's integrity, you might as well walk away. Personal pride will prevent the negotiation from leading to a mutually agreeable price.

- In many countries the haggle game is expected, even when you're buying fruit on the street. Although you may have purchased the same article before and you know the right price and vendors know you know, they still want you to do the dance. It can be frustrating, but be patient, keep your cool, smile and press for the proper amount. If that fails to produce satisfaction in a short time, walk away or pay. Anger and reasoning will get you nowhere.

- A two-tiered pricing system for locals and tourists is a reality and you shouldn't let it bother you. It may not be fair in most people's eyes, but it makes good economic sense. Prices in the marketplace will reflect what the market will bear. The two-tiered system works most against you when you look too interested or too affluent. It's true that prices are often adjusted to what the buyer appears able to afford.

- Be extra cautious when purchasing expensive items. Give yourself time to shop and practice your negotiating skills on less expensive items first.

- There is no magic formula for determining a fair price, such as countering with half the asking price. Vendors long ago caught on to this feeble attempt at circumventing the necessity of research and have adjusted their prices accordingly.

- Try not to let your day-to-day budget be the final determiner of what is affordable. Something costing the equivalent of a week's living allowance may look like a bargain when you're back at home. If you've come upon a once-in-a-lifetime opportunity to buy something of lasting worth and can make the necessary adjustments to your budget, go ahead and buy.

- Avoid making purchases at congested tourist sites. Vendors there are less inclined to give you a deal because some wealthier tourist is sure to be close behind.

- The best deals can be found where competition is highest and often that means where large numbers of shops sell similar items. Use this leverage to your advantage.

- If you are interested in buying several of the same item, buy the first at the best price you can obtain. Find another shop with more of the same item, inspect quality carefully and casually let it be known that you purchased one from another vendor. The second vendor will probably ask how much you paid and may quote you a lower price because he doesn't expect you to buy.

- An agreeable but disgruntled shopkeeper is no guarantee you got a good deal.

- The cliché "Time is money" is true for merchants. The more time they invest in a sale the more they need to make the sale. Remember, however, that the same principle applies to buyers.

- Involving a supposedly antagonistic partner can be an advantage to you in bargaining. You express interest in buying at a certain price, but the partner disapproves. You offer to consult with your partner and return to the vendor with an offer less than asked but within reason. Chances are the vendor will agree to finalize the sale.

- When bargaining for expensive items and and getting no satisfaction from the clerk, ask to deal with the person in charge. Bosses have far more autonomy to offer a final price and may even be motivated to close the sale by the prospect of losing a little pride in front of their subordinates.

- Presenting the correct amount of cash to back your offer may encourage vendors to accept it.

- Try to learn to read numbers in the local language. It will come in very handy where prices have been posted.

- If all else fails in negotiating a good price, and you have the advantage of time and patience, return to a shop a number of times in the effort to win the shopkeepr's agreement through sheer persistence. But don't expect this tactic to work unless you keep your encounters upbeat and brief.

"If this is your first time in the USSR you are welcome to it."
– Sign in Moscow hotel

Managing Money

 Every overland journey on a shoestring budget involves a preoccupation with saving money. The preoccupation grows as your financial reserves decline. Even those with a good supply of cash often take pride in their financial resourcefulness on the road. Saving money, however, can become an obsession. If every opportunity for new experience becomes limited by worries about money, burnout is inevitable. A well-planned budget will relieve much of the stress, and you will certainly discover ways to conserve cash without compromising your experience.

Tips for Trips

◪ Share transportation and lodging, if possible. A double room is usually only slightly more expensive than a single, and two or more people hiring a taxi or renting a vehicle will save at least 50 percent of the going rate.

◪ If possible, stay with family and friends en route. Remember that good guests are courteous, do not take their hosts and hospitality for granted, clean up after themselves and around the house, offer to help with some of the bills and try not to upset the routine of the household too much. This behavior will leave them wanting to see you the next time, and you can offer to return their generosity at some time in the future. Remember, though, that contrary to what many people believe, staying with acquaintances along the way is only cheaper than staying at a hotel when you are in a very expensive city or if you are a very cheap guest!

- Buy an airline or railway pass giving you unlimited use for specified periods.

- A student card, if available to you, is great for cheap rates on transport, sight-seeing and lodging. Black-market student cards are available in many cities along the overland route, but quality can vary.

- In Latin America, some restaurants offer a set lunch called *Menu el dia* ("menu of the day") or *Almuerzo*. It is usually quite simple, filling and cheap. Just find an empty seat and join in!

- Consider purchasing a car with a few other people and selling it before moving on. But you must be aware of all insurance restrictions placed on this kind of joint purchase.

- Duty free purchases such as alcohol and cigarettes can bring you a fair profit on the black market in countries where they are restricted or difficult to obtain. Ask other travelers as you go.

- If the country you visit has cultural or religious ties to you or your family, you have a wonderful opportunity to make new friends with similar values while saving on expenses.

- Some places of worship and education (monestaries, temples, universities and so forth) have been known to take in travelers, providing them with limited lodging and the possibiliy of free courses of instruction. There is, however, no official means of identifying such people. You simply recognize opportunity if it arises.

- Many tourist information centers offer free maps and other valuable information.

- Cutting hair, drawing portraits and busking (playing a musical instrument for change) have helped many an overland traveler subsidize a meager budget.

- In cities famous for resorts, there are probably more upscale tourists than overland travelers. If you dress accordingly, it is easy to blend into the scene and get the benefits of the pool or entertainment facilities of a large hotel while staying at an inexpensive one.

- Purchasing weekly transit passes is cheaper than taking a taxi.

- If staying in a place for long period, ask your hotel manger for a free or discounted room if you bring the hotel more business. Many people are happy to trust the advice of another traveler when getting off plane, train, bus or boat in an unfamiliar location.

Changing Money

One of frequent routines of overland travel is changing money. Typically you have several options: banks, money changers, hotels and the black market. Shop around the banks. Some have better rates and charge smaller transaction fees. Money changers offer a less favorable rate but have better hours and may be more convenient. Hotels have the worst exchange rates but will do when options are limited. The black market offers the best rate but puts you in a position of compromise by the very nature of its relation to an underground industry that is neither regulated nor policed.

I was in transit at the train station in Sarajevo and needed something to drink. I spotted a vendor on the platform and purchased a soda. Back in my seat, I calculated the exchange rate and realized I'd given him US$14 for a can of pop! I went back to confront the man and with a shrug of his shoulders, he gave me the correct change. – CARYL

If you are changing money with someone who does not share your language, bring out your calculator. Have the person punch in the appropriate numbers and then do the same in return. It is important to rely on your own figures. Once you have received your local currency, ensure you count it in front of the money changer. Once you are out of sight, the transaction is over. Bills in large denominations, such as fifties or hundreds, generally bring a more favorable exchange rate. In return never take worn, ripped, faded or tissue-thin bills. It will be difficult to find someone to accept them. The advantages of cash over traveler's checks seem to depend on the country and market.

I dutifully counted the small stack of notes passed to me by a teller at a money exchange in Acapulco. After calculating the transaction myself, I showed her she had made a mistake in her favor. She retrieved the stack, recounted it, recalculated the number and added a few more bills to the stack. I counted the bills again and, sure enough, it was still short. So I took her calculator and worked out the transaction in front of her and then counted the money again. She finally shrugged her shoulders and gave me the proper amount without any hint of remorse. – WAYNE

Black Markets

Black markets have developed around the world as a means for the general population to gain access to consumer items that are unavailable on the open market or heavily taxed or restricted by government. When it comes to money the same definition applies. Locals who need to raise hard currency to travel abroad or buy goods on the world market get a much more favorable exchange rate if they do it on the street, cutting out all the red tape and bureaucratic middlemen.

If you wish to deal on the black market for currency, talk to the locals and other travelers about the degree of caution you should use. In some countries the black market is a legitimate parallel, and all transactions are completed in the open with no real threat of prosecution. In other countries the black market is illegal. Assess the local situation carefully before using the black market.

TIPS FOR TRIPS

- ◪ You do not have to look for the black market—it will find you.

- ◪ Cash is usually all that the black market accepts. American dollars are in highest demand.

- ◪ Know what the local currency looks like. Many countries change the design of their currency often, and you do not want to get stuck with worthless out-of-date paper money.

- ◪ Use common sense when engaged in a black market transaction. Stay away from secluded areas and groups of money changers who persist in trying to do business with you.

- ◪ It is always safer to exchange money at a permanent location such as a store or established business.

- ◪ Never hand over your money until you have counted and have in your hand the local currency.

COMMUNICATION

Friends of mine set up a website of their ongoing world travels and designated someone to maintain and update it while they were gone. Photos and stories were sent home regularly for all interested parties to see, and those wishing to correspond with the travelers could do so directly through the website, eliminating the need for exchanging cards or letters, which could take weeks. It was so cool! A website of your travels is like an e-zine for everyone to enjoy. – WAYNE

Calling Home

Although satellite and telecomunications technology has improved dramatically in the last decade, phoning home from remote locations can still be difficult and expensive. Some countries have long distance direct capabilities, which connect you to an operator from the country of your choice. From there your call will become a local collect one, bypassing any extra rates or charges.

Some countries do not have phone direct capabilities because people calling overseas are a lucrative source of income for the government and phone company (which are often the same entity). In such cases all calls must be paid for in the country of origin. To get around this problem you have three options: use an internet café to access your e-mail, find a fax machine or use a private phone. A one-page fax typically takes around a minute. You will save considerably on phone charges while paying relatively little for the service charge. You can typically also receive fax transmissions for a similar per-page fee. If no fax machine is available, find a private phone and familiarize yourself with all the restrictions placed on incoming calls. Try to arrange to have a caller from home contact you at the private phone so the charges are paid for back home.

Tips for Trips

- ✐ If you have a phone credit card, let the phone company know you are traveling overseas. The company may need to verify why so many calls are being made out of your regular phoning routine or inquire about a substantial increase in its use.

- ✐ Take precautions when using your card so criminals known as shoulder surfers cannot intercept your access numbers and use them to make calls that you may very well be responsible for.

- ✐ If there is a need to stay in touch regularly, but not necessarily to speak, you can always use the old standby of calling collect and having the people at home decline the charges.

- ✐ If you call person to person you can sometimes leave your phone number so the other party can call you back.

Sending Mail

Take mail and postcards to the post office and have the postage canceled (stamped) in front of you. Otherwise, uncancelled stamps can be removed and resold or used again by someone else. When mailing postcards, buy the necessary stamps first and stick them on the card so you can determine exactly how much room is available for writing. Many times, your writing ends up half-covered because of the size or number of stamps.

Be creative when sending postcards home. Just about anything you can put a stamp on can act as correspondence. I've seen a coconut mailed from Hawaii (not that I would recommend it). I've also heard of sending exotic beer coasters with your writing on the back. It works and can be more interesting than a postcard. Use your imagination. – WAYNE

In Nairobi, Kenya, I went to pick up my mail at the post office. My mother had sent some homemade cookies, and although they arrived a little broken, they were a delightful surprise and a great taste of home cooking. – CARYL

Receiving Mail

Receiving mail while on an extended trip will at the very least provide a welcome break in the overland routine. It may even bring a tear to your eye and a lump to your throat. Getting a letter from home can do wonders for the morale, especially in cases of travel burnout.

If you plan to receive mail abroad there are several options besides the fax. Poste restante, the mail service offered by American Express and your hotel are the three most common. Anyone can use poste restante, but you must be an AMEX client to take advantage of their service.

TIPS FOR TRIPS

◪ Inform those writing to you that they should address envelopes and cards with your surname first, underlined, because correspondence is filed alphabetically under the first letter of your last name.

◪ Instruct them to write the complete address:

Your last name (underlined) followed by first name
Poste Restante
Main Post Office
City
Country and Continent

◪ Use major urban centers for your mail drops because the facilities and service are probably better than in smaller centers.

◪ Be prepared to search for mail filed under every conceivable variation of your name and the sender's name.

◪ Establish a post office box at home where people can write and have a designated person pick it up and forward it to you. Thus, everyone can write to a central location while only one person needs to know where the correspondence has to be sent.

◪ It is possible to get mail forwarded when you leave a country. By paying a small fee and filling out a form, you can have your letters redirected to an address you request.

I received a letter from my grandmother nine months after it had been mailed and a few months after she had died. Amazingly, it had been through seven cities on two continents before I finally received it, but her final words to me meant the world. – CARYL

163

Shipping Purchases Home

Before shipping anything home, go to the point of conveyance (post office, airport, shipping lines or broker) and obtain all the information you need about packing and sending your shipment. Sometimes, for example, customs regulations require that the shipping company or agent examine the contents of the package before it is sealed.

Tips for Trips

- Find a suitably sized box of heavy gauge cardboard. Wrap breakables and place them in the center. Fill excess space with paper or some sort of cushioned packing. Then prepare a card with all address information and a list of the contents and their value. Place the card inside, on top of the contents, before closing. Seal the top and bottom with sturdy packing tape. For added structural support run a strip down all corners. Finally, write the address in indelible ink on the box.

- Acquire a sack or nylon bag, which can typically be found in shops or the marketplace. Some may be specially designed for shipping, but bags left over from food stuffs such as rice or flour will do just as well. If you cannot locate a suitable sack, purchase some plain cotton or calico fabric and have it sewn to fit the dimensions of the box.

Too many words for a postcard. It'll have to go letter rate.

- Cut off any excess fabric and sew it together, double stitching for strength.

- Fold and double stitch the top and bottom of the package. Then apply sturdy packing tape.

- Write the destination address on both sides and list how many boxes are in the shipment (for example, box 1 of 3).

Overland Transportation

Overland transportation can get you from one place to another and offer an unparalleled view of a country's landscape. But foremost, it is a great way to experience a country's culture.

I was traveling with some friends who were on a trip around the world. They were booked on a flight connecting in Bombay to the Middle East, but reports of heat, poverty, overcrowding and threats of disease made them wary of staying over for a few days in India. While discussing their dilemma, another traveler, more familiar with India, wisely suggested that if they really wanted to experience the country, they should do it from the inside of an Indian train! It would not be clean or comfortable, but the Indian railway system offered the safest, quickest and one of the most effective ways to experience the country and its people up close. – WAYNE

THE LONG HAUL: BUSES AND BOATS, TRAINS AND TRUCKS

Anyone traveling for an extended period will eventually have to take a lengthy overland journey. A long trip gives you the opportunity to settle in, watch the scenery, get to know other travelers and reflect upon all the experiences you have had.

Overland travel in India can be a never-ending source of frustration, even when traveling a popular route such as the one from New Delhi to Agra, the home of the Taj Mahal. Familiar with the delays typical of Indian bureacracy and leaving nothing to chance, I arrived three hours prior to departure time to purchase my ticket. At the main ticket booth I was told the train was leaving an hour earlier than I thought and that I had to go to the tourist ticket booth. After waiting in line there, I was directed to yet another booth. The heat was stifling, the station was overcrowded and my backpack weighed forty pounds. I fought my way to the counter of the third booth only to be told that my ticket had to be purchased back at the tourist booth and that the train now left two hours earlier than I had anticipated. I elbowed my way back to the tourist ticket booth where an official said, "I cannot sell you tickets to Agra here, but if you go to the main ticket center, they can sell you one there." Back where I had started, I encountered the same official who had started me on my wild goose chase around the New Delhi train station. He recognized me immediately and realized I wouldn't leave this time without the correct information. He cheerfully sold me a ticket to Agra and the train left at its originally scheduled time.
– Caryl

Tips for Trips

- When considering transportation to your next destination it is always best to check the availability of a seat as far in advance as possible.

- Ticket counters in developing countries are inevitably crowded and chaotic, requiring tolerance, patience and strong elbows. Some locations offer special facilities for tourists, but where these are unavailable, you'll have to wait and endure or hire someone to stand in line for you for a small but well-deserved fee. This service can be arranged through your hotel or a local travel agency.

- When purchasing tickets for trains and buses, always check arrival times. Just because one train or bus leaves earlier than another does not mean it will arrive earlier; it may be a milk run or may follow a longer route.

- If you are leaving a country, buy a ticket only to the border and then continue your journey on the next country's transport. This is usually less expensive than buying a ticket in one country to take you to a destination in another.

- Purchasing a ticket does not always guarantee a seat, especially on buses. All it guarantees is that you can board the bus and go along for the journey.

> *Three friends and I purchased seats together for a bus trip to Manali, India. My friends found their seats clearly marked with their appropriate numbers, but a gentleman was sitting in my seat. I informed him politely of the situation and showed him my ticket number. He responded that the number on the seat had been rubbed off and that he was not, therefore, in my seat. I argued that because he was sandwiched between seats ten and twelve, and the seats were in order, he must be in my seat, number eleven.*
>
> *He looked at me and in all sincerity said, "Yes, ma'am, but in India there is no order." What more could I say? I stood for the entire journey.* – CARYL

- Keep your cool in the crowds of kids who invariably frequent train and bus stations.

- Be aware of religious or civic holidays and do not venture out unprepared. Tickets for overland transportation may be unavailable or transports may be packed, depending on the holiday.

- River travel through some countries is possible only in the rainy season, when water levels are high.

- Some countries issue rail passes to foreigners and will hold a quota of seats available. Passes, however, are usually economical only if you are in a country for a short time and have many miles to cover.

- Never leave the platform while waiting for a train or bus to depart.

- If you are boarding a train and the lights go out, take extra precautions to guard your baggage. If you are not settled in a seat, get off until it is safe to reboard. If you are not yet on the train, stay off until the lights come on.

- Use a combination lock and bike cable to secure your pack to the luggage rack or another fixed object.

- Carry all valuable, expensive or breakable articles in your day pack. Never let your day pack out of your possession.

- Make sure that heavy window shades are properly secured if raised. They can come crashing down on your hand or arm, causing serious injury. Sliding windows can also be a concern.

- Traveling at night saves hotel costs, but you miss all the scenery. And the night's rest you get often leaves a lot to be desired.

- When traveling by overnight train, spend a little more money and get a berth (often called a sleeper). You'll arrive in better condition. The top bunk is a good choice because it can be used as a retreat during the day if you wish to lie down and you can keep your bags with you, away from moisture, garbage and thieves.

- When resting in a berth, lie with your feet facing the front of the train. If there is a sudden stop, you don't want your head to cushion the blow.

- Nobody dies from motion sickness. If you suffer from the problem, try to seat yourself in a place that minimizes disturbances: close to midship on boats and near the center on buses. Eating light, bland, low-fat snacks before and during a trip will reduce the severity of motion sickness. Getting as much fresh air as you can, keeping the movement of your head to a minimum and fixing your gaze on the horizon also will help. Cigarette smoking and reading won't. Commercial remedies must be taken before symptoms emerge. If you're feeling sick, it's already too late.

- When traveling by bus in tropical regions, check behind the driver's window for red stains, which indicate that the driver chews betel nut. Betel nut, the astringent kernel of the seed from the betel palm, is chewed by many in the tropics. Chewed with lime and mustard-seed pods, it turns a bright red and produces a mild numbing or narcotic effect. To avoid being splattered with it, sit on the other side of the bus if possible. If not, try to keep your window closed. Betel nut stains are almost impossible to remove from clothing.

- If you are not traveling with a trusted companion, carry all unsecured valuables with you when leaving your seat, even for a moment.

- Train toilets usually drain directly onto the track, so take special precautions to ensure nothing valuable can fall in.

- Keep your windows and shades closed when entering or leaving a station to prevent being robbed or grabbed. This is especially important for women.

- In certain parts of the world, there are trains just for women. These can be as enjoyable as co-ed compartments.

- If, for whatever reason, you decide to join locals atop the train or bus, secure yourself with a strong rope or belt fastened to something that will hold your weight in the event of an unexpected roll or fall.

- Do not be alarmed if your rail car gets unhooked from the rest of the train; it's not unusual for a train to be divided at some point along a journey. Notice of the ultimate destination of your car should be posted on the outside. If not, confirm the destination of the car with the conductor.

- If a train is running behind schedule, it may not stop as long as it should at a particular station.

- There are generally three places to store your bags on a bus, depending on its make and class: on top, inside on a rack or in a separate luggage compartment beneath the bus. No matter where your luggage is stored, you should always be in a position to watch the loading and unloading to make sure your bag gets on and gets off when you do. It is always wise to use a pack cover to protect your belongings from the elements.

- Your carry-on pack should be stocked with a full bottle of safe drinking water that can be replenished at rest stops, a small provision of food in the event of delays, a small towel for clean-ups and a roll of toilet paper.

169

◪ If your destination is a very small town, or if you arrive during the night when most passengers are sleeping, there may not be a public announcement. So it is your responsibility to know where to to get off. Ask the conductor, driver, ticket taker or a fellow passenger to advise when you've reached your destination. It is also ideal to keep a map handy and check off stops along the way.

◪ If you decide to really rough it, you can often travel by truck. You can get a ride by hitchhiking, but it is best to obtain a ride at a local truck stop, where you can negotiate a price, which should be lower than bus or train fare. If you are unsure of that price, check around with other travelers. Try not to pay until you reach or are near your destination. If there is a problem or a breakdown along the route, you will be able to get out and find an alternative form of transport to complete your journey without paying the full fare, which, in most cases, is non-refundable.

◪ Do not be surprised if there are other riders. Some may be friends of the driver or other paying customers. This is normal in many circumstances.

◪ Traveling on an open truck bed is a great opportunity to get fresh air and see the countryside, but take precautions against the elements. Sunglasses and a bandanna are essential.

While traveling in India through the northern Himalayas, I caught a lift on top of a truck cab for two days. The road, seldom traveled by foreigners, was accessible only four months of the year. I got the view, the photos and the ride of a life-time. – CARYL

LOCAL TRANSPORTATION

Local travel in developing countries can range from the familiar taxis and subways to the unfamiliar auto rickshaws, motorcycles, pickup trucks, rickshaws, trishaws and even donkey-drawn carts.

You name it—if it can be adapted to carry people for a profit you will see it on the street. These ingenious modes of transport can range from quiet to ear shattering, from dangerously fast to relaxingly slow, from environmentally friendly to environmental disaster. They are usually very inexpensive, so be adventurous. Step right up and take a ride. It's all part of authentic cultural experience.

TIPS FOR TRIPS

◪ In congested urban centers, subways are often the most inexpensive and effective way to get around. The availability of weekly passes can make the subway an even better bargain.

◪ Taxis are more expensive but also more convenient, especially when you don't know your way around.

◪ Never accept a ride in a car that is not clearly marked as a taxi.

◪ Research cab fares to desired locations. Settle on a price with the driver before departing. If the driver tells you the meter doesn't work, there is a good chance he may either be attempting to get you to pay more than the metered rate or to keep the money for himself instead of paying his employer. Always reconfirm the price before paying.

◪ Countries suffering from rapid inflation may have special taxi conversion cards designating the new rates since it is difficult to reset many meters. If this is the case, discuss the situation and negotiate the fee with the driver before departing.

◪ Cabbies are usually a good source of streetwise information, but don't be too friendly. They may want to become your personal chauffeur during your stay.

◪ Ensure that your luggage is stowed safely in the trunk of a taxi. Many times trunks are secured only by a string or bungee cord. Do not trust the driver to make sure it is secured. Test it yourself.

- Take lots of change for taxis because the drivers will probably tell you they don't have any.

- Try to keep track of significant landmarks so you will know if you have passed a place more than once on the same ride.

- If you feel you have been deceived or duped, you can complain and pay, or attempt to negotiate a fair fee.

- Hire a cab for a half-day or full day to familiarize yourself with the layout of the town.

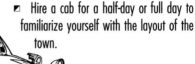

I've heard of one man who went into partnership with a local cabby to drive him around to all the shops that paid the driver a small commission even if the tourist didn't buy. After a day of driving around to more than thirty shops, they split the profits and parted company. – WAYNE

- If safety on the road is a concern, you can give drivers a financial incentive to drive slowly and safely. Inform them that reckless driving will earn a specified amount less than what was agreed upon. Firmly tell them they get one warning.

- Group taxis are good for day-trips or for traveling short distances out of town. They can be more comfortable and convenient than other forms of transportation, but usually you'll have to wait until every seat is filled before leaving.

- The truly adventurous may want to rent a motorcycle, scooter or car, but if you will be doing any amount of driving you should consider getting an international driver's license and insurance before you go.

- Most rental agreements require payment by credit card.

- Read the terms of the rental agreement carefully to determine your insurance coverage. Some credit cards provide collision coverage on vehicles. Before leaving home, you can also check with your car insurance carrier to see if your policy covers rentals in foreign countries.

- ⬛ Carefully inspect the vehicle for damage and have it noted on the agreement form before leaving the lot. You don't want to be charged for damage you didn't do.

- ⬛ Carefully inspect the vehicle to ensure that lights, tires, brakes, windshield wipers, heating or air conditioning, and engines are in good repair.

- ⬛ If you are renting a motorcycle, ask if there is an engine kill switch to be used in an emergency.

- ⬛ Completely familiarize yourself with controls and instruments before venturing into traffic. Then take a day or two to get used to driving the vehicle in local conditions before taking any lengthy road trips.

- ⬛ Record the vehicle description and license plate number and keep this information among your personal documents on your person in case the vehicle is stolen.

- ⬛ Do not pay for vehicle repairs out of your own pocket because you may not be reimbursed. Call the company collect and ask for a replacement vehicle or instructions on vehicle repair.

- ⬛ License plates or stickers that identify rental vehicles are an open invitation to theft.

- ⬛ Check the back seat of your parked rental car for intruders before getting into it.

- ⬛ Criminals may follow rental vehicles from the airport, force them from the road in a remote location with the intention of robbery.

- ⬛ Poor visibility, crime, animals and pedestrians on the road make traveling at night hazardous.

- ⬛ On multi-lane roads, the lane closest to the center is best for general security.

- Keep car windows closed, doors locked and valuables out of sight at busy or suspicious intersections.

- Anything of value left in an unattended car should be locked in the trunk before you reach your destination.

- Don't park a vehicle near anything that could conceal potential thieves.

- If you must stop to ask for directions, do so in a busy, well-lit area.

- Staged accidents are not uncommon in many countries so do not stop to offer assistance. Drive on and notify the authorities as soon as possible.

- Park rental vehicles off the street at night, preferably in a lighted garage with an attendant or at least behind the walls of your hotel. Use your own padlock to secure motorcycles and scooters.

- Before venturing out on a rented motorcycle or scooter, ensure you are protected with a helmet, long pants, full jacket, sunglasses or other eye protection and leather boots. Short sleeves and pants, sandals and unprotected heads are an open invitation for a hospital stay. If you can't obtain proper attire, don't rent a motorbike or scooter.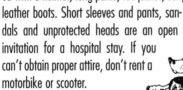

- Motorcycle riders must take additional special safety precautions because they are not as visible as larger vehicles, and because they are more affected by road hazards such as potholes and animals. Motorists may attempt to pass you with little regard for your safety, and large trucks may create a draft sufficient to force you off balance. Oncoming vehicles may move into your lane, and motorists may be more inclined to cross intersections in front of you. Rain, especially in the first few minutes, can be particularly hazardous before oil, grease and dust have been washed off the road. Finally, speed does not mix with motorcycles overloaded with cargo and passengers.

- If you have any lawsuits to lay against a rental company, see if they have an office in your home country and do your suing from there.

- A horse and buggy ride through a city can be very romantic, but check the condition of the animals before hiring. Many locals do not have sufficient income to feed their families, let alone a working animal. If you do take a ride, support the drivers who value their animals by taking good care of them.

I decided to rent a motorbike to drive through the Northern part of Thailand. I wore a helmet, and as a cautious and defensive driver, I was ready for anything. I set off on the highway. The first encounter with two lanes of traffic becoming three wasn't so surprising, except that all the vehicles were coming directly at me! I had to slow and drive off the roadway. Three vehicles continued to drive right past me. That fearful first encounter prepared me for driving a motorbike in Thailand. – CARYL

HITCHHIKING

Hitchhiking is a great way to break up the monotony of using public transport (in fact, hitchiking *is* a form of public transport in many countries) while spending some time with people you would normally never meet. But for this same reason, hitchhiking also should always be considered dangerous, especially for women traveling alone.

Waiting for a lift...

175

Tips for Trips

- Hitchhiking is always much more successful if you look presentable and stand in a visible location that gives drivers plenty of room to pull over.

- The hand signal for hitchhiking varies from country to country. Make sure you know what you are communicating.

- Don't be shy about attempting to convince a vehicle to stop. Look the driver in the eye and smile. Be animated. Make a connection.

- Hitchiking can be a slow form of transportation, so budget plenty of time for getting around.

- Carry a sign stating your destination. When all else fails, try writing the word *please* in the local language.

- If you have no luck on a major highway, get off onto a smaller road and try there. People are more likely to stop at slower speeds. Also, they probably don't see hitchhikers all that often and may be more interested in stopping for you.

- When you get into any vehicle, open the door once or twice to familiarize yourself with its operation in case you need to get out in a hurry.

- Be prepared to talk to drivers. They are usually picking you up for company.

- If you are asked for payment, negotiate a price or get out and try again. If money is not requested, then it is polite to offer to buy drivers a drink or some food or perhaps a little gas. Use your discretion.

- Travel light so you can get in and out of vehicles with little effort. The driver shouldn't have to open the trunk to stow your gear.

- Always be careful when leaving the car at rest stops if your gear is still inside. If you don't have a companion to stay with the vehicle, take your gear with you.

- Never cross a border with a stranger who has given you a lift. Likewise, never cross a border with someone you have picked up. In many countries, if your ride or guest is guilty of anything, you are guilty by association. Terminate the arrangement before reaching the border and cross alone. You can always join up on the other side if you wish.

- Darkness has a way of coming quickly when you are stranded on the road.

Always wait in locations where shelter or lodging can be obtained if you get stuck without a ride. Also, carry sufficient food and water.

If hitching in Europe, you may be interested in contacting Allsop (an association made up of the clubs Allauto, Provoya and Stop-Voyages). It is instrumental in linking drivers with those willing to share fuel costs. An annual membership fee of US$25–$35 provides you with unlimited access to cost sharing car or truck travel information for one year or you can pay for one-time use.

There are Allstop offices in Canada, the United States and in major centers in France, Germany, Denmark, Spain, Switzerland, Austria and England.

I once hitchhiked to Key West, Florida, from Miami. The first ride I caught was going the distance. I could tell the driver had been living in it for some time with all the fast food take-out boxes and garbage piled up in the back seat. I asked him a few questions about his circumstances and he managed to address any suspicious concerns I had until we reached our first service station in Key West. I went inside to wash up while he filled the car with gas. When I returned he was heading down the highway with all my gear. I was dumbfounded how easy it was for him to do that and kicked myself for giving him the chance. Luckily, I had all my valuables safely stashed in my passport belt-pouch and we were on an island with only one road out. I called the state police, and they apprehended the man shortly afterward. My bag was returned with an eye opener of a lecture on hitchhiking from the officer, who had some pretty shocking stories to tell of people less fortunate than I was. I got off easy on this one, but I will never let my guard down again. – WAYNE

Trouble on the Overland Route

Seated in a taxi in the markets of Dar Es Salaam in Tanzania I had a thief open the car door and rip some gold chains right off my neck. I ran after the thief, who, luckily for me, slipped and fell. Some locals who had witnessed the theft started to kick and punch the man as I stood in disbelief. Two policemen approached the scene, but rather than arresting him, they joined in with their clubs. I was horrified. Then, from the corner of his eye, the thief saw me and stretched up his open hand, which contained the chains. I quickly took them and retreated to the taxi. As the cab started to move, one of the policemen knocked on the window and asked if I wanted to press charges. "No," I said, "just let him live," and we drove off. – CARYL

Crime is an ever-present fact of life at home or on the road, but you tend to be more conscious of it when you travel. This is good unless it drives you to paranoia. Although there is no foolproof way of keeping yourself from becoming another victim of a determined, clever, sophisticated or desperate criminal, there are many things you can do to reduce the possibility.

The first thing to remember is that most crime requires opportunity. When you are not in control of yourself and your surroundings, you become a target. Like wolves, criminals follow a profile and separate their victims from the rest of the pack. Thieves look for people who are confused, fatigued, looking for adventure, overloaded, flashing their

179

valuables, careless with their money transactions, alone in dangerous areas, awed by scenery or just plain distracted. Regardless of your condition, you must be alert to potential threats. Increase your security by listening to the precautions of honest locals, other travelers and by studying your destination guidebook and surroundings. You will eventually develop an ability to sense potentially dangerous situations and to act accordingly.

Whether they're casual cheats and hustlers or hardened professionals, criminals cannot always wait for people to inadvertently make themselves vulnerable. Sometimes they need to create the opportunity. This can be accomplished in as many ways as can be imagined, but all have one thing in common: to get your eyes and mind going one way while your valuables are going the other. Nigerians have an expression: "If you have too many things to take care of at any given moment, you will soon be relieved of that responsibility."

I was buying a couple of tickets at the advance ticket counter for the evening train out of Bangkok. The ticket agent said, "That will be nine hundred baht." I said, "Fine," and began to get the money out. He then asked if I wanted two tickets, and I said, "Oh yeah, two please." He then said, "Eighteen hundred baht please." It wasn't until later that I looked at one of my tickets and saw printed in tiny but readable numbers, "450 Baht." – JOAN, UNITED STATES

Professional thieves are the same everywhere. Some will even rely on violence to get what they want. If you are held up by a person with a weapon, do not resist. Remember that it takes about four pounds of pressure to pull the trigger, and a finger resting on the trigger supplies about two pounds. There is not much you can do when confronted by thieves with weapons but comply and attempt to escape unhurt. You can, however, avoid leaving yourself in isolated situations where weapons can be brandished openly.

Situations involving theft through cunning and skill are more common and harder to avoid. Your best weapon against them is prior knowledge about the typical scams, cons, and stings found on the overland road.

Scams, Cons and Rip-Offs

Confidence Scams

Confidence men and women are the front line of fraud. Sent out to snare potential victims, they can be seen in any area where tourists and business people hang out. They pass themselves off as legitimate business people with important ties to tourist industries or perhaps even government. They are usually well dressed for their roles and may even carry a briefcase or cellular phone to bolster their image.

The most skilled never walk up to you directly unless you appear to need assistance. Usually, they will place themselves in a position to initiate casual conversation. Once confidence people have your attention, they will begin to manipulate the conversation. They will ask superficially innocent questions through which they determine your interests, weaknesses or vices. With knowledge of these, they can adjust the scam accordingly. But invariably it will involve a deal that's too good to be true.

The bait for their scams can involve any number of things such as carpets, antiques, art or gems. You will be skillfully manipulated to the point that you will more than likely be the one who suggests doing business. Confidence people may even go so far as to lend you money for a short time in order to gain your confidence and draw you deeper into the scam. Always question people's motives, and if you don't feel right about any situation, move on.

My partner and I had just arrived in Bangkok and were on our way to Chinatown. We were checking a map for directions when a well-dressed, professional-looking man approached to ask if he could be of assistance. He told us he worked with the Thai government and had the day off because of a national holiday.

After directing us to Chinatown he engaged us in a few moments of polite conversation. He asked us where we had been, what we had seen and if we had made any purchases. With that information he suggested a few places of interest in Chinatown. If we were interested in buying gems at a below wholesale cost, he said, today was perfect because of the official holiday and the opportunity to circumvent government regulations. As a matter of fact, he had a very good friend who owned a gem shop. If we liked, we could take a look. Of course, there was no obligation to buy. He hailed a cab, gave the driver his card and directed the driver to the shop. We figured we had nothing to lose, so we went.

When we arrived, the driver escorted us to a doorman, who showed us inside. We were impressed. This was a posh shop with many sales people and sparkling display cases containing an array of jewelry. The owner greeted us. She was in her midfifties, well spoken and carried herself with an air of cultured confidence. We told her about the gentleman who had directed us to her shop, and she invited us into her office to have a drink. We were relaxed and enjoying a respite from the heat and confusion of the streets outside.

The owner began to show us a variety of expensive gems, which we expressed no interest in buying. We should not buy them for souvenirs, she told us, but for profit. Because of the government holiday, she could make a sale at an extremely low price. If we sent them out of the country before the next day, we could circumvent the usual export taxes. She would give us the address of a buyer in Holland who would pay twice the price. This one little venture could pay for my entire trip twice over. I didn't have cash on hand but she assured me that if my credit card allowed cash advances the deal could be done.

We spent the next hour choosing the best stones for export. I was sent off with a driver to five banks to withdraw the necessary cash. Back at the gem shop the package was sealed with wax and my signature and official-looking documents were attached. The driver then took us to the post office where we mailed the insured package special delivery.

Later that night, at our hotel, when the excitement and adrenaline had cleared, we started to question our judgment. At the hotel front desk we learned there was no Thai government holiday that day. We started to relate our story, but the clerk gave us a look that indicated we need not continue. He had heard the same story so many times he could finish it word for word himself.

He told me I had been duped and should contact the Bangkok tourist police, which I did immediately the next morning. They informed me there was little they could do unless I had the gems in my possession.

After all, it was no crime sell a customer nearly worthless gems regardless of promises of a quick profit. Buyer beware and all that.

I went to the post office and demanded my package back. I learned that the package was being held in a special bonded area to which there was no access. Not to be deterred, I worked my way around the building until I found someone who I thought could help me. Bribes and intimidation didn't work, but he agreed to a game of Ping-Pong at lunch hour when nobody was around. After the game he offered to retrieve my package. Now I had to get my money back.

I returned to the tourist police station and pressed them to provide me with an officer to accompany me to the gem shop. The owner of the shop was surprised to see me return with the police and a bitter exchange followed. Eventually, she offered me a partial refund. I had invested US$2,000 and received a refund of US$1,700. An expensive price to pay for a little bit of experience. – MATT, ENGLAND

Card Game Scam

Card games are a popular diversion on the road and an ideal opportunity for con artists to reel you in. You are befriended and invited to watch a card game. During the game your escorts lose money. After it is over they claim to have discovered that the winner cheated them. They plan a revenge match to cheat the cheater. You're invited to join and win some big money. Of course, it doesn't work out quite that way, and you will be the big loser in the end.

Traveler's Checks Sold and Reported Stolen

Someone offers to buy your checks at a percentage of their face value, instructing you to report them lost or stolen and to get a full refund. It may sound simple and foolproof, but the moment you enter into any kind of larcenous enterprise you leave yourself open to prosecution and all that comes with it in a foreign country.

Squeeze Play

In a crowded place, such as a market, train station or lineup, the person in front of you stops suddenly, letting you run into him. He then elbows you, steps on your toes or does something else to get your attention. Those walking behind naturally press into you, creating a crush of people. Because your attention is diverted by the person in front, you do not detect the pickpocket's fingers in your pockets or bags.

The Sneeze

In a crowd, a person behind you suddenly sneezes all over your back. When he appologizes and proceeds to wipe it off, he or somebody else is also going through your pockets. Other substances smeared as a decoy on your back or bag may include mustard, soap, ketchup or anything messy.

Money Drop

Money can be a tremendous inducement for distraction. To divert your attention, a thief points to some money under your seat or near your feet. As you reach for the money or discuss its ownership, the thief's partner in crime is reaching for your belongings.

Thieving Children

Children can grow up fast and hard on the streets, becoming skilled thieves at a very young age. They may attempt to sell you something or overwhelm you with sheer numbers, but the object is to divert your attention while your pockets or bags are picked. A common ploy is for a few children to gather round you and press cardboard or a stiff newspaper into your midsection. While you fend them off, an accomplice goes through your pockets or bag.

Monkeys

Monkeys are very intelligent and can be trained to do many things. In some places they have been trained for larceny. Your hotel room may be safe from humans but there are still plenty of opportunities for monkeys to gain access. And yes, they do know what to steal. If not, they have been taught to open the door for their owner, who enters and cleans you out.

Phony Police or Officials

If you are stopped by someone in what appears to be a legitimate uniform, make sure you are in the presence of a *bona fide* official. Ask to examine identification, and if there is any doubt, consult with a legitimate local business person. Do not let the so-called official choose a person to verify his identity because the two may be working as a team. Unless you are absolutely certain of the legitimacy of the person, do not accompany him to a police station or let him accompany you to your room. Under no circumstances surrender your passport unless you are at a legitimate police station.

Weighed Luggage

You are approached in a crowded bus or train station by what appears to be an official who questions you about your destination and informs you that your bags must be weighed before being placed on board. Convinced that the person is a legitimate employee, you hand over your bags only to watch them disappear into crowd.

Hotel Staff Theft

Hotel staff may remove something of value from your pack and hide it in a drawer, under a dresser or on a shelf in the hope that you won't notice it when leaving. As long as the hidden item remains in your room, no one can be accused of theft. Once you check out, hotel staff return to your room at their convenience and remove the item.

Phony Brand Name Products

In some countries, a regular con has to do with selling cameras or other electronic equipment with brand name shells (or bodies) and inferior guts and mechanisms. Even if you've checked all parts for authenticity you should beware that a switch doesn't happen when the product is being wrapped.

Careful local, Peru

A merchant offered to give me a deal on a Minolta lens because it was a shelf demo. Later, I noticed it was not a real Minolta lens but a very clever copy with a slightly altered trade name. I stormed back to the shop, but the shopkeeper refused to refund my money, claiming he had never represented the lens as a Minolta and the true name was written on the receipt (in a language I didn't understand, of course). I had no legal recourse except to inform the tourist police, who said it would take a week to pursue the matter. So I had to extend my trip to receive a refund from an extremely disgruntled shopkeeper. – Brian, New Zealand

187

Hobson's Choice

This form of theft happens in stations or anywhere tourists are likely to congregate. You're alone with your bags sitting on either side of you. Two men approach, and one grabs the smaller of your two bags. If you chase the man with your smaller bag, the other man walks off with the larger one.

Black Market Money Changers

Thieves patrol tourist areas impersonating money changers and rely on your inexperience and fear to pull off their scam. You complete a transaction, having counted the currency. The money changer suddenly becomes nervous, telling you that the police are watching. He requests his money back, returns your dollars and suggests you leave quickly to avoid being busted. He hopes you will clear out before counting your money because the top bill is real while the others are singles or phony. The same can happen with the local currency if the deal is quickly concluded when the so-called police are looking away for a moment.

Calculator Short-Change

Thieves posing as money changers offer to exchange your currency or traveler's checks for local money. They use a reprogrammed calculator to determine a cheaper rate of exchange and cheat you for a portion of what you are owed.

Drug and Rob

It's not entirely uncommon to be befriended on a journey and offered a little refreshment only to wake up later with your valuables gone. There have even been reports lately of prostitutes coating their genitals with sleeping drugs. After the intimate event, the man falls asleep and the prostitute walks away with his cash.

*I had been traveling for about a week with three com-
panions I met on the road. The night before two of us
were to leave we were invited for tea in the room of the
others. I awoke the following afternoon with a
migraine. My possessions were gone and my traveling
companion was in the hospital in a coma. When the
police investigated they found a few of my companion's
belongings under my bed, and I was charged with theft
and attempted murder. The charges were soon
dropped, and our naïveté was gone with our money
and gear.* – JAMES, AUSTRALIA

Dishonest Travel Agents
You are offered a great price for a seat on a charter, but
you have to make a nonrefundable deposit. If, as may well
be the case, no seat is available on the flight your deposit
will be lost if you do not apply it to a higher fare. A variation involves paying for a ticket in one city with instructions
to pick it up in another at a later date.

Lotto Winner
It's remarkable how the promise of easy money causes
people to hand over their common sense along with their
funds. A typical scam involves a man who approaches you
with a lotto ticket, saying he has the winning numbers but
cannot pick up the prize for some bogus reason. He wants
you to buy the ticket for a very reasonable price. How can
anyone be so gullible? It does happen.

Shell Game and Three-Card Monty
The age-old shell game and its lesser-known playing-
card derivative persist because they work. They both
involve a dealer and at least two accomplices. In a crowded
tourist area the dealer of the three-card monty variation sets

up a table with three cards bent in the middle and standing on edge so the faces aren't showing. He gathers a crowd, shows them one card, shuffles them about and asks for bets on its final location. His accomplices immediately place bets and win. When the tourist crowd begins to smell easy money, the con is on. At its extreme the scam may even involve an accomplice marking a card to make its location obvious while the dealer is presumably distracted. When the dealer returns to the game and begins shuffling the cards, the tourist bets go down hard and fast, only to be followed by a collective gasp when they all lose. At this point it's common for another accomplice to cry that police have suddenly been spotted nearby, and everyone scatters.

Hold My Baby

You're sitting in a crowded location such as a train or bus station with your bags at your side. The lady sitting beside you is trying to handle her baby and bags at the same time. She asks if you would mind holding her baby for a moment. You lean over to oblige and in the blink of an eye her accomplice rushes off with your bags.

Bait and Switch

A popular scam on the street is bait and switch. It can happen as easily in a store when an item is taken into the back (or out of your sight) to be wrapped up and then substituted with an inferior product or, worse, no product at all. But the easiest place for the bait and switch to happen is on the street. A hawker will approach you and show you an impressive item. The bargaining dance takes place and when you are near what the vendor feels will be the most you will pay, he'll wrap it in a bag with a few knots to make it secure and then hand it to you with his final price. You say no, he takes his bag back, stuffs it in his shoulder bag and turns in frustration to walk away. After a couple of steps (but never out of your immediate sight) he turns around as if he has had a chance to think about it, reaches into his shoulder bag and pulls out the bag your item is in. He then hands it back to you and agrees to your last offer. The problem is that the item in the bag he is giving you is not the item you were initially bargaining for. If the knots are not untied and the product checked before payment takes place, you will not know you've been ripped off until you get back to your hotel room.

Pickpocket Warning

When passing a sign warning you of the presence of pickpockets in the area, resist the urge to immediately check your passport pouch and pockets. The warning sign is a ploy offering thieves an opportunity to locate your most valued possessions and, soon enough, to relieve you of them.

Clumsy Tourist

This mild form of extortion involves blaming you for a minor accident in a market or restaurant that results in damage to the other party's property. The value of the damaged goods will be inflated, and you will be pressured to pay. The situation may also provide a distraction for an accomplice who is a pickpocket.

Tips for Trips

- Do not argue with a thief with a weapon. If held up at knife or gunpoint, hand over your valuables immediately.

- During your first few days in a new setting, do not engage in negotiations for purchases. Wait until you are more familiar with prices, local scams and potential danger spots.

- Do not attempt to make purchases through the window of a train or bus stopped at a station. Too many things can happen to your money when it's waving out the window and to your bags when you're distracted.

- The confusion and commotion created when boarding trains or buses provide perfect opportunities for thieves.

- Never accept the assistance of porters unless you are certain they are legitimate.

- Always carry your shoulder bag on the shoulder opposite the curb. Motorcycle snatch-and-rides are common in large cities.

- If photo permits are required by law, be suspicious of locals or tour guides who say it's okay to attempt covert photographs. They may be informers setting you up for a police shakedown.

- Public displays of wealth are an invitation to thieves. Never wear expensive jewelry.

While exploring a busy bazaar in Cairo, I noticed someone following me and a female companion. We stopped for a moment, but the culprit ducked out of sight. Her expensive gold earrings may have been the cause, so I suggested she take them off. Unfortunately, she didn't. Not long after, a thief skillfully removed them. She was lucky his dexterity spared her physical injury. – WAYNE

- Never rest or hang anything of value on restaurant chairs, bathroom doors or any place that is vulnerable to fleet-footed thieves.

- Never walk alone late at night. Take a cab. If you think you are being stalked, duck into a shop and wait or call a taxi or police.

- Bootleg, or knock-off, copies of brand name products are available on the streets of just about every major city in the world, but now even *copies of knock-offs* sell on the street for the price of knock-offs but offer even less value than the poor-quality first generation replicas.

- While learning to yell "stop thief" in the local language is helpful, yelling the word "fire" may get attention more quickly.

- Be careful of groups of children trying to sell you newspapers or trinkets.

- A person occupying your prebooked seat on a bus or train may be a distraction for a pickpocket.

- Avoid conversations with large groups of unknown people, where you can easily be set up for scams.

- Refuse unsolicited help, especially while shopping. Likewise, do not acknowledge requests from strangers until you know your belongings are secure.

- In tightly packed crowds, always hold your day pack securely in front of you.

- Conduct all financial transactions discretely to avoid the possibility of thieves learning where you carry your cash.

- When carrying spending money in your pockets, place small bills on top.

- For added security, strap your bag or fanny pack under clothing.

- Masseuses or massage therapists offer great comfort to weary travelers, but they are sometimes great covers for scam artists, so be wary.

- If you have been duped by an unscrupulous merchant and are unable to get a refund, try taking a picture of the person as a last resort, but only if it's clearly safe to do so. Sometimes the prospect of photographic evidence makes the merchant more willing to deal with your complaint.

- Paying for an airline ticket with a credit card may result in the number being recorded on the ticket. If the ticket is subsequently stolen, the thief will have access to your credit card number.

- Any transaction that must suddenly be rushed should arouse your suspicion.

- If you are being held up and want to attempt a quick escape, try throwing your wallet in one direction while running in the other.

- In a physical encounter, try to keep your bag between you and the assailant.

- Always carry a small amount of accessible money so you have something ready to hand over in the event you are robbed. Having no money to give may incite violence.

- Always carry a stash of US$50–100 somewhere secure in case everything else gets ripped off.

- Locals will sometimes point to their eye to alert you to watch your possessions.

- Never travel alone in game parks or on treks that thieves and bandits have been known to frequent.

- Stolen valuables sometimes can be repurchased for a nominal sum at a local market known to feature stolen goods. Remember that the person selling you your own property is not typically the thief.

- If any of your valuables are stolen, get a police report so you can claim it on your insurance when you arrive home.

- Be wary of invitations to enjoy someone's hospitality unless it is clear who will be responsible for paying. Many times people, including other travelers, will try to take advantage of your friendliness and feign poverty or a misunderstanding when it comes time to settle the bill.

- Exotic nightclubs may have additional charges that you aren't aware of until the bill arrives. Upon entering, make sure you know exactly what you will be charged for.

- Stories about money needed for moral or political purposes are typically scams.

- Children may demand that you hire them to wash or watch your rental vehicle. If you refuse to pay, chances are good that something will be damaged or missing by the time you return. Negotiate a fair price beforehand or park in a more secure location.

- Never accept a stranger's invitation to have your picture taken with your own camera unless you are sure you can run faster.

- Never accept a service unless the fee is firmly negotiated beforehand. You may be setting yourself up for a mild form of extortion.

- Men should never go into a strange woman's room. She may attempt to extort money by threatening to accuse the male of rape.

- If you are resting while alone, it's always best to secure your bags to something solid with at least a sturdy strap or, better, a bicycle cable and combination lock.

- Always check your hotel room thoroughly before leaving.

- Always be careful when accepting food or drink from people on any form of transport, especially if you are in a private compartment. Many travelers have partaken in a little refreshment, only to wake up a few days later with a splitting headache and all their valuables gone. If you are unsure about accepting offers of hospitality, feign illness or allergies.

ILLEGAL DRUGS

One word: Don't! Buying dope in an exotic location may be one of the most exciting and dangerous things you could ever do on a trip. But it's not worth the consequences if things go wrong. No matter how secure a situation may seem or how low-profile you think you are, your life and future may be in serious jeopardy. Better to err on the side of safety. Do not get involved. If you insist on indulging against every authority's better judgment, here are some things to remember:

- In some countries, you are categorized as an international trafficker, regardless of the amount.

- Never carry drugs across the border for yourself, for profit or for a friend. Always be certain what is in your bag and never let anyone else use your excess luggage allowance.

- A drug's potency is never really known until it is ingested.

- In particularly popular areas for drugs, always check any new hotel room for anything illegal that may have been hidden and could be located during a routine drug raid and assumed to be yours.

- A good lock on all zippers of your pack will help discourage police from planting anything while you are not watching.

- Never take the seller back to your hotel room or let him know where you are staying. The seller may be setting you up for a shakedown.

- Never let a seller take you too far away from a safe and secure area.

- Be discreet. Never assume it is okay to indulge in the open. Popular hippie travel spots may seem safe, but there is always the threat of a raid. (Besides that, smoking dope in the open is about as disrespectful to the local culture as nude sunbathing. Sometimes it is tolerated but never accepted.)

- Social smoking (sharing the same smoke) is a good way to contract communicable diseases.

- It is best to distance yourself from junkies and people who may be involved in questionable activity.

- Keep in mind that police may pose as dealers and bust you once you buy.

Most of all, be aware of and sensitive to the host country's attitude toward dope. Sporadic crackdowns or waves of arrests may be common in order to make a false "political" statement of commitment to dealing with the drug problem. Every bust, no matter how small, can be used to further a political point. Use your head and a little common sense in any situation that places you at odds with the laws or morals of a country. It's your choice as well as your responsibility.

BUSTED

No brush with the law in a foreign country, especially a third world country, will leave you feeling nostalgic, but being arrested for buying or selling drugs is a guaranteed bad trip (pun intended). Once arrested, your uncertainty and anxiety will be fueled by a growing sense of abandonment. After all, you are in a strange country with a strange legal system, and you may not even know the language. To add to your troubles, your time in jail will probably not be spent in a comfortable holding cell. Many third world jails are everything you've been told and worse.

TIPS FOR TRIPS

- In many countries you can be found guilty by association. Choose your company well. Stay away from demonstrations, even peaceful ones that could result in your arrest.

- Never sign any police document you do not totally understand. You could be signing a confession, or, worse, you could be admitting to a crime you know nothing about. Answer questions, but make no admissions and volunteer no information.

- In many developing countries, vehicle accidents are automatically blamed on any foreigners involved, whether it is their fault or not.

- In retaining a lawyer, choose not the one with the best education or command of English, but the one with the best local connections.

- If you are incarcerated, try to find someone on the outside to bring you food, money, medicine, clothing, blankets and so on when needed because you can almost guarantee that the authorities will not provide anything but your confinement.

Incarceration: Legal Contacts

For nationals of:

England
Prisoners Abroad
Telephone: (country code +) 0171-833 3467

Holland
Bureau Buitenland
Telephone: (country code +) 73 612 32217

Ireland
ICPO (International Commission for Prisoners Overseas)
Telephone: 1 872-2511

Canada
Foreign Affairs
Telephone: (613) 996-8885.
In countries without a Canadian consulate, contact an Australian or British embassy.

If you are from any other country, you should contact your closest consulate to inquire about hiring a lawyer, contacting family and friends, ensuring you receive fair treatment (according to the standards of the country you're in) and, if applicable, extradition home. Be aware, however, that consulate staff will not provide you with legal advice, representation, or bail.

International Legal Defense Counsel
24 Fl. Packard Building
111 South 15th Street
Philadelphia, PA. 19102 USA
Telephone: (country code +) (215) 977-9982

> *An American arrested in Columbia obtained the services of two lawyers on the recommendation of other inmates. After paying for the lawyers' services, he was poorly represented, convicted, given a significant jail term and had no opportunity for appeal because his lawyers had vanished. International Legal Defense Counsel was able to recommend a legitimate lawyer who exposed a fraudulent kickback scheme with inmates and two individuals not even licensed to practice law in Columbia. Luckily the case was retried, but in most cases the victim gets no second chance.*
> – RICHARD ATKINS, INTERNATIONAL LEGAL DEFENSE COUNCIL

BRIBERY

Bribery is the grease lubricating the wheels of many foreign bureacracies. Also known as *baksheesh*, backhander, dash, payoff, payola, *el soborno*, *la mordida*, *wairo* and *bustarella* (to name a few), bribery may make you uncomfortable, but it is a reality, and at some point in your travels, you may face the unpleasant challenge of dealing with it. Situations inviting bribes may arise at borders, embassies or other shrines of officialdom that you must pass through. Even if you've done your homework and know the policies regarding border crossings, commercial goods, visa restrictions and so forth, what they say in the capitol and what they insist on at the border may be completely different. Sometimes, only *baksheesh* can set things right. How you handle yourself will go a long way toward determining the outcome.

Bribes are of two kinds. The first is passive, a soft bribe involving little personal risk except your time and frustration. The second is more serious. It is a bribe of defensive preservation better known as the hard bribe. In this case you risk deportation, a prison sentence or losing a large amount of money.

Soft Bribes

It is inevitable that some encounters with government officials will result in denied requests or at least delay in granting requests. In most cases, a bribe is not expected. Be patient and polite, and give officials the opportunity to bring up the issue of *baksheesh* themselves. If they don't, and they continue to deny or delay a legitimate request, you may have to take the initiative. Find a discreet way to let them know you are willing to pay a little more than the normal service fee to expedite your request. If they balk, do not push the issue. The last thing you want to do is insult officials. If their response is truly a ploy, they will let you know before you reach the door.

After it has been discretely established that money or gifts will change hands, the process is similar to bargaining and may even be cordial. If you have done your homework you should know roughly how much *baksheesh* is required. Have that amount readily on hand and be prepared to bargain for it. Don't lose your composure, and don't let it become personal. What's bribery to you is a way of life to the officials. If skillful bargaining fails to result in mutual satisfaction, it is time to become more assertive and insist on speaking to a superior. Lesser officials are not likely to want things to go that far since the more people involved, the smaller the share per person.

Whatever the outcome, inform fellow travelers so they can better prepare themselves. Above all, remember that any irregularities in your documents, possessions or manner will draw attention and invite the prospect of larger bribes.

In Lukla, Nepal, my knees gave out while trekking to Mount Everest, and I needed to catch a plane back to Kathmandu. Unfortunately, the government had closed the airports for five days (nobody knew why), and a huge backlog of passengers had developed.

To my advantage I had been in town long enough to get to know the locals, including the air traffic controller. I approached him to inquire about the cost of getting one of the first flights out of town. I discretely let it be known that I was willing to pay if the price was right. When he asked if traveler's checks or cash would be involved, I knew I had the makings of a deal. I was on the first flight back to Kathmandu. – CARYL

Hard Bribes

If you keep your nose clean and observe the laws of the country you are traveling through, there is little chance of having to deal with a hard bribe.

Two Canadians entered Brazil with fake passports even after being warned against it by fellow human rights

*activists. Their known connection with political organi-
zations resulted in their arrest for kidnapping and extortion, and their fake passports became key pieces of evidence against them. They were found guilty and are now
serving fifteen- to twenty-year terms in a Sao Paulo hell
hole, hoping for extradition back to Canada.* – WAYNE

You may find yourself in the wrong place at the wrong
time and be unjustly detained. Do not mistakenly think
that you can wait until you are in a police station or in front
of a judge to explain your innocence. You won't. The
wheels of justice turn excruciatingly slowly, especially in
third world countries. As long as you have not been locked
up, there is a strong possibility that you can buy your way
out quickly and quietly.

In the beginning, officials may intimidate you with physical or verbal threats. At this point they will likely let you
know in no uncertain terms that you are in very big trouble
and had better realize the gravity of the situation. They will
inform you of a fine, penalty, jail term or worse. They will
ask for or already will have your passport. They also will
more than likely search you and your luggage. They may
even attempt to physically drag you off, which you should
resist without appearing confrontational. Above all, however, try to remain calm, diplomatic and in possession of your
cash. Refer to your antagonists by their rank or position
instead of calling them "Sir," a term often reserved in third
world countries for servants when addressing a superior.

If by this point you are not in custody and on your way
to the police station, you are probably being set up for a
hard bribe. If circumstances are desperate and you are little more than the victim of extortion, you may have to meet
their demands. If not, the opportunity for negotiation may
exist.

While writing a freelance article on American prisoners in foreign jails, I interviewed an inmate doing time in an Afghan prison. The interview was recorded on a micro-cassette recorder I smuggled into the prison in my underwear. I was searched more thoroughly when leaving, and my recorder was discovered. It was confiscated, and I was told to leave. I insisted on the return of my property, wanting more than anything the contents of the tape. Eventually, I was taken to the office of a superior, where I pleaded my case. I said I hadn't been informed that cassette recorders were forbidden. Hearing this, he cracked a B-grade movie smile, walked me over to a window, pointed to the notice board at the main entrance and translated the message in heavily accented English: "No electronic equipment."

I made one last attempt, pointing out that the official looked like a reasonable man and promising that the offense would not occur again. The official knew full well he could have me tossed out on the street or into his prison. He smiled playfully again. "You have balls! I like that!"

He held up the recorder and said, "You would risk confronting me for something as easy for you to replace as this. But what is of true value to you?" He extracted the tape. "I am a reasonable man and will give you a choice. You can have this," he said, referring to the recorder in his left hand, "or this," referring to the tape in his right. "But remember, no matter which you choose, you will not be allowed back unless you plan on staying with us for a long time."

Without a moment's hesitation, I took the tape, gave him two backup batteries and bid him farewell.
– Chris, United States

BROKE BUT NOT DESTITUTE

Finding yourself penniless in a foreign country can strike even the most roadwise with panic, but it does not have to. If you run short of funds for whatever reason (theft, lost possessions, bad planning, to name a few), you must gather your wits about you and deal with the problem quickly. The first order of business is to secure a place to eat and stay, so you can deal with restocking your depleted reserves. You may want to offer your labor in exchange for food and lodging, but if you do not find a sympathetic ear, try contacting your country's embassy or expatriate community, where guidance, if not assistance, may be offered. Short of that, you may solicit the help of religious or social organizations such as CUSO, the peace corps, missionaries, priests, the Salvation Army or local institutions such as temples or mosques.

Once you know where your next meal is coming from, money can be raised doing odd jobs in restaurants or bars, locating customers for hotels, cutting hair for other travelers or even street performing (if you have any talents or musical abilities). Observing how locals engage in business also may provide inspiration.

Regardless of how you earn your keep, remember that the kindness of strangers merits your genuine appreciation. A presentable appearance and heartfelt thank-you can make a potentially uncomfortable situation easier on everyone.

If all your efforts fail to raise funds, you will have to consider leaving the country. Under such circumstances, you may present yourself to the embassy of your home country for deportation. You may also contact someone at home or at your country's embassy for a short-term loan to return home. Of course, any deportation expenses or loans will need to be settled shortly after your repatriation.

I was flying into Singapore from Indonesia with a travel partner, and we were low on cash. We had US$60 between the two of us—just enough to get to Kuala Lumpur, Malaysia, where our next instalment of travel funds was waiting. An immigration officer asked how much money we had to declare, so we explained our situation. He told us the funds were insufficient and we would have to return to Jakarta in the morning— but in Jakarta we would be thrown in jail for having no Indonesian entry visa!

Not knowing what else to do, we called the Canadian consulate. Within the hour an official from the embassy arrived with something called a writ of assistance, which provided enough money to support our stay in Singapore for two weeks (our parents back home took care of reimbursing Ottawa). The the immigration officer gave us a one-week visa and said, "Welcome to Singapore." – WAYNE

Coups D'état

If you are in a major city during a coup, stay indoors and never travel on the street until your safety is assured. Above all, never travel after dark because soldiers are often ordered to fire on anyone who defies the curfew that will inevitably be in effect. The first forty-eight hours will be the most dangerous, but if hostilities last longer, you must concern yourself with obtaining water and food while considering options for escape. Contact your embassy at the earliest opportunity.

If you are unfortunate enough to be caught in the middle of gunfire without cover, lie down with your arms over your head. Do not look up until the shooting has subsided and you can escape to safety. If you are in a building when the shooting starts, stay away from windows, turn out lights and lie on the floor as far away from windows as possible. If possible move to an interior bathroom or stairwell.

Hijacking

The chances of becoming involved in a hostage taking are extremely remote, but if it happens you must be prepared for an often lengthy ordeal that will tax your psychological and emotional resources to the limit.

Tips for Trips

- The most dangerous phase of a hijack and hostage taking situation is usually at the beginning, when terrorists are most determined and irrational.

- Don't try to be a hero. You may endanger yourself and others.

- Don't resist or make sudden movements that could be interpreted as threats.

- Do not try to escape unless you are certain of success.

- Try to remain inconspicuous. Avoid direct eye contact and any appearance of observing your captor's actions.

- Avoid alcoholic beverages.

- If interrogated, keep answers short and don't volunteer information. Avoid political and religious topics. Give innocuous reasons for traveling and never admit to accusations. Minimize the importance of your occupation if it could be politically sensitive or make you a high-profile hostage. Comply with all orders and instructions. Other hijackers may be covertly mixed in with the rest of the passengers so be careful what you say.

- If you are held captive for a lengthy period, try to establish a rapport with your captors. Ask them to refer to you by name. Show a family photo and appeal to their feelings for family and friends. Maintain your sense of personal dignity and gradually increase your low-key requests for personal comforts.

- Establish a daily routine of mental and physical activity. Think positively and avoid succumbing to despair. Remember that you are a valuable commodity to your captors. Keep your mind active. Keep a journal even if you are not allowed to retain your writings. If material is not available, mentally compose poetry or fiction. Try to recall scriptures or designs of houses. Perhaps even play mental tennis, as one hostage did.

- ◪ Loss of appetite and weight is typical, so it's essential to make a conscious effort to maintain your health. Eat what is offered even if it doesn't look or taste appetizing.

- ◪ If drugs are administered, do not resist. Sedatives are sometimes given to make you more manageable.

- ◪ Unobtrusively make mental notes of your captors and surroundings. The information you remember will be valuable later, especially if you are selected for early release.

- ◪ If authorities attempt rescue by force, stay low and do not make any sudden or suspicious moves that could identify you as a threat.

SURVIVING A PLANE CRASH

Airlines are correct in telling you that it is safer to fly than to drive. Statistically, ten thousand people would have to fly ten thousand miles each year for fifteen hundred years before a plane was due to crash. But in that crash, chances are high that lives will be lost.

Preparations for surviving a crash begin before you leave the ground. Listen to the flight attendant's safety instructions. Familiarize yourself with emergency instructions contained in the card in your seat pocket and mentally plan your escape route.

TIPS FOR TRIPS

- ◪ If a crash is imminent, put on your shoes to protect your feet during impact and escape. (You must, however, take them off before using the emergency slide.) Secure your seat belt firmly around your hips and assume the crash position: head on your knees, protected by your hands, with your elbows pressing your legs together.

◪ Chances of surviving impact are good if the fuselage remains intact, but the threat of fire is high. The fireball will melt the windows in seconds, spreading smoke and flames throughout the cabin. Keep low and crawl toward the exit, which should have its path illuminated by emergency lights on the floor. Even these, however, may be obscured by smoke. If you have planned your escape carefully, you should be able to count the number of seats to your nearest exit.

◪ Once you are out of the plane, move away in case of explosion. Tend to injured passengers, if you are able.

◪ On flights over water, make sure you are familiar with the location and operation of life vests and rafts.

EARTHQUAKES

Typically, travelers receive ample warning of most natural disasters such as hurricanes and floods and are able to leave the area or take precautions. There is often, however, no advance warning of an impending earthquake, and you must take action to ensure your safety.

TIPS

◪ Conventional safety rules suggest that you remain inside a building during an earthquake due to the high probability of injury from falling debris. But every situation needs to be assessed individually. If buildings in the immediate vicinity are only one story and the building you are in is constructed of clay, rock, adobe or concrete, then you will probably be safer on the street.

◪ If you remain inside a building, duck under a sturdy piece of furniture like a table or desk, cover your head and neck, and hold on to the furniture so you are not shaken free from your cover. If cover is not available, drop to the floor and crawl to the nearest inside wall or doorway, which have the strongest structural support. Take care to stay away from windows and objects that might fall on you.

◪ In a crowded facility such as a stadium, you will have a better chance of survival if you don't panic to escape. In this situation you are more likely to be trampled to death than injured by the quake.

- If you are outside in an open area, stay away from power lines, cliffs and embankments. If you are outside in a metropolitan area with tall buildings, get to a doorway as quickly as possible, and shield yourself from breaking glass. Protect your eyes by pressing your face firmly against your arm. It is estimated that the downtown of a large modern city may have more than one meter (three feet) of broken glass raining onto the streets below from high-rise buildings.

- Expect aftershocks. Take measures to relocate yourself to a safer area if necessary. Above all, stay away from rivers, which may be prone to flooding and mud slides after a quake. If near the ocean, move to higher ground because an underwater quake can result in a tsunami (tidal wave).

- Avoid entering buildings after a quake because of the high possibility of structural insecurity and leaking gas.

Adventure Travel

TREKKING

If it's true that traveling on a budget often brings the greatest rewards, then trekking, which can be virtually free, is an adventure not to be missed. Before leaving on a trip involving some serious trekking, expect to do some serious training, especially if you will be at high altitudes, where the oxygen is thin and fatigue sets in very quickly. Once you are on location, do not get carried away by your sense of adventure and attempt too much too fast. Preparations should include at least a modest cardiovascular and muscle-building regime.

In Nepal one is constantly trek conscious. The guest books and notice boards of traveler haunts are filled ad nauseum with glowing descriptions of newly discovered trekking possibilities. All a bit much. In response I penned "Trek to Room D" in a mountain cafe in Dhu-

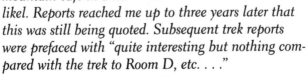

likel. Reports reached me up to three years later that this was still being quoted. Subsequent trek reports were prefaced with "quite interesting but nothing compared with the trek to Room D, etc. . . ."
— TONY JENKINS, *TRAVELLERS TALES*

The Trek to Room D

*This is a much overlooked but very pleasurable trek
and not nearly as arduous as that of Namobuddha or
Panauti. From the restaurant it can be combined with
a short trek to the toilet to make a full and interesting
day. It is recommended you have good footwear (a sturdy pair of thongs) and perhaps an umbrella or poncho
as the weather may take a nasty turn. It is best to set
out before 5:00 P.M. so as to be back in plenty of time
for supper.*

*Starting from any table in the restaurant, pro-
ceed on the level of the doorway (north
wall, fairly centrally locat-
ed). You may encounter
friendly waiters en route
who can direct you. Once
through the door the trail
leads down the steps to the
flat central courtyard. A
sidetrack to the toilet can
be made from here. Just
carry on straight for a
while. The toilets will
appear in a line before
you. They are clean and
fairly recent, but only of
some interest to stool buffs.*

*Proceed onward keeping the clothesline on your left
and in sight. The route goes up a small but steep step
and through the door to the central lodge. Those
fatigued can find a rest area here, and drinking water
is near at hand. This may be a good spot to have a
light snack and a breather before tackling the steep
ascent of the stairs. This climb some find daunting,*

*but press on as a view from the window of Room D is
something of a privilege to experience.*

*It is seven or eight stairs up to the first landing.
Drinking water is also available at this stage. The route
turns sharply, cutting back across the landing before
rising another eight stairs to the rarefied air of the second floor. It was at this stage that the French expedi-
tions of '53 and '55 were lost. Once past, the way gets
much easier though there is not yet a banister so one
must be careful of their footing. From here it is smooth
progress slightly left across the landing and on to the
door marked 'D.' You have arrived! Now go to bed you
lazy bastard!* – TONY JENKINS, *TRAVELLERS TALES*

Supplies for Treks

Nothing is worse than finding yourself many miles into
the wilderness without an essential item, so plan accordingly for the terrain, weather and duration of your trek. The
following is a list of essential gear to which you can add
items necessary for local conditions.

☐ Sleeping bag.

☐ Tent.

☐ Cooking utensils, stove and fuel.

☐ Route map, which shows facilties along the way, and
compass.

☐ Food and containers.

☐ Water purification chemicals or tablets.

☐ Sturdy waterproof footwear and clothing for all types of
weather. Always break in boots before beginning a trek.

☐ First-aid kit, sunscreen and insect repellent.

☐ Moleskin or Band-Aids for unexpected blisters.

☐ Sturdy bags to pack up garbage.

☐ A sturdy walking stick.

☐ Flashlight with extra batteries, quality camping knife and rope.

TIPS FOR TRIPS

- Always let someone know where you will be trekking and when you plan to return.

- When shopping for supplies, consider weight, convenience, ease of preparation and the amount of garbage created. For example, glass containers are heavy and subject to breakage.

- Your pack will always be heaviest at the beginning of your journey, when you are carrying the most food and are not yet fully acclimatized. Try to eat the heaviest food first.

- For best weight distribution, pack your bag high on your back, not low on your hips.

- Consider renting ponies, yaks, mules or porters to carry some of the heavier gear.

- Before leaving, check the weather forecast and consult with guides and police about potential natural or human dangers.

- Dress in layers. Women should consider wearing a loose, midlength cotton skirt, which is cooler in warm weather. In cooler weather, pants can be worn underneath.

- Keep your feet dry and in good shape. Attend immediately to any signs of tenderness or blisters. Keep toenails trimmed, use foot powder, wash your feet often and expose them to fresh air and sunshine. Routine foot massage will increase your comfort.

- To dry your boots, hang them upside down on a stick. To dry socks, pin them on the outside of your backpack while walking during the day, or slip them into your sleeping bag at night.

- Eat full meals in the morning and evening and snack throughout the day to keep your blood sugar level constant.

- Walking downhill can be harder than walking up. Let gravity take you, but control your rate of descent and try not to build up too much momentum. If your downhill walking style is too restrained, you can overwork unused muscles and cause fatigue and stiffness the next day.

- Avoid slippery or loose terrain. A slip with a full pack can prove disastrous.

- Pace yourself and give your body a chance to acclimatize to conditions. Walk only as fast as the slowest person in your party. Be realistic and tolerant.

- If your feet get mired in a bog, lie on your back to distribute your weight and pull one leg out at a time and roll out of the soft area.

- Stop to make camp well before dark. To quickly estimate the time before sunset, hold your flat hand sideways in front of you with the thumb up. Count the number of fingers between the bottom of the sun and the top of the horizon. Each finger will be roughly equal to fifteen minutes. For example, if you count three fingers, you have approximately forty-five minutes until sunset. You will need to experiment with this method to take account of season and latitude.

- Expect to experience the symptoms of acute mountain sickness (AMS) at heights of greater than 3,000 meters (9,750 feet). The shortness of breath, slight dizziness, mild headaches and loss of appetite should subside after a few days. If they don't and you begin to feel intense breathlessness, a dry, irritating cough, severe headaches, prolonged loss of appetite, nausea and vomiting, it is time to stop and recuperate. Try descending to a lower altitude (even 500 meters [1,625 feet] may be enough). If symptoms persist, try the medication commonly known as Diamox.

- It is important to not mask the effects of altitiude sickness, so do not take aspirin for headache relief.

Camping

"Camping on the sand is forbitten!" a sign on a beach on the Island of Ios, Greece, warned us. Disobeying the obviously misprinted warning, we laughed and proceeded to set up a makeshift tent. But after four nights and a million sand flea bites later, we wondered if the sign was truly a misprint after all! – SONJA, SWITZERLAND

- Don't camp close to streams or rivers, which can be subject to flash floods.

- Do not store food in your tent or backpack overnight. Suspend it from a tree if possible.

- No natural water source should be considered safe. Always purify drinking water with purification tablets or chemicals.

- If you must leave you bag outside at night, leave all pockets open, so rodents won't chew holes while exploring.

- Remove the tops and bottoms of empty cans to make them easier to crush and pack out.

- In jungles, it's essential to store your pack off the ground so it does not absorb moisture and invite unwanted guests.

- Garbage that can't be burned must be packed out.

WATER SPORTS

No matter where you travel, chances are good you will end up near water. Although there are advantages and disadvantages to every environment, water seems to always bring with it a relatively healthy local population, refreshing weather patterns, sufficient food and abundant recreational possibilities.

TIPS FOR SWIMMING

- Be thoroughly advised about local conditions before entering the water and always let someone know where you will be swimming and when you plan to return.

- Swim only in sheltered locations such as a bay or cove. Before entering the water take note of currents by watching for floating debris and other swimmers. Swimming with the current will reduce fatigue.

- Wear footwear in waters containing coral, rocks, sea urchins or other potential hazards.

- Both surface currents (riptides) and underwater currents (undertows) can be deadly because they may be strong enough to pull you out to sea. If caught in a strong current, try to swim parallel to the shore until you escape it. If the current is too strong to fight against, conserve your energy, relax, don't panic and wait until you feel its momentum subsiding.

TIPS FOR DIVING AND SNORKELING

- Avoid taking malaria pills if you know you will be diving because they can cause spacial disorientation. Consult a physician.

- Pack your diver certification card and logbook.

- Thoroughly check any diving gear before venturing out.

- Many diving boats do not have protection from the sun, so bring sunscreen, a hat and a long-sleeved shirt.

- Reef fish will eventually accept you as a part of the environment if you remain still with your arms folded and your feet motionless.

- Question dive-boat operators about their experience and knowledge, and examine their boats for seaworthiness before booking. Check ease of entry into and out of the water, toilet facilities, navigational equipment and freshwater storage, first aid and protection from the elements.

- Do not hire operators who anchor directly onto reefs. Ask the dive master if he anchors on secure mooring.

- Be careful not to damage the coral with any of your equipment.

- Handling marine life stresses it and may even be dangerous. Ask your dive master about regulations governing the feeding of wildlife.

- Never stick your hands into small caves or crevices because they are often the home of dangerous creatures such as moray eels.

- If you experience nausea, breathing difficulty, vomiting or intense swelling after being stung by a sea creature, seek medical attention immediately.

- Always avoid jellyfish, even if they are dead on the beach, and always wear a wet suit where jellyfish are abundant. Jellyfish can be minuscule and almost invisible or large and obvious. Contact will result in symptoms ranging from mild stinging that may produce welts like bee stings to severe pain and shock. Though painful, contact with jellyfish is not usually life threatening, except in the South

Pacific, where box jellyfish stings can be fatal. If jellyfish are abundant in your location, consider purchasing a commercial sea sting kit. Do not rub fresh water or sand on a sting because it may release more toxins into the skin. Vinegar will reduce additional toxin discharge, and antihistamines or analgesics will help relieve itching and redness. Meat tenderizer or ammonia will help reduce pain and promote healing. In severe cases, seek medical treatment immediately.

▪ Sea urchins are round bottom dwellers whose spines cause great pain. The spines are brittle and must be removed completely and carefully with tweezers. Baking soda or shaving cream will make spine removal easier. Vinegar diluted lime juice or ammonia will help reduce pain.

▪ Contact with corals and sponges leaves behind spicules, which can be removed by applying a piece of adhesive tape to the affected area and tearing it off. Vinegar will help reduce pain.

▪ Stingray, catfish and starfish stings can be treated by soaking the affected area in hot water for about an hour. The fins of catfish and spines of starfish produce the same kind of venom, so the hot water treatment is also effective for these stings.

TIPS FOR WHITE-WATER RAFTING

▪ Hire only experienced guides with a good reputation and safe equipment. Minimum raft equipment should include life jackets (one extra per raft), rescue rope, first-aid and repair kits, spare oars and paddles and survival equipment.

▪ Before taking to the river, ensure that you thoroughly understand emergency white-water procedures and rescue techniques.

▪ Dress appropriately for weather and water conditions.

▪ Wear shoes to protect your feet if you are thrown overboard or need to walk for help.

▪ Be especially careful when you are on the downstream side of the raft because there is greater danger of being trapped between the raft and rocks.

▪ If you are thrown into the water, float on your back with your feet facing downstream to protect you from running into rocks. Head for the shore as soon and as safely possible.

Working Abroad

Working abroad is a wonderful opportunity to encounter a country and its culture in a far more intense way than traveling through it could ever afford. To work legally in most countries, you will require a work visa or permit, and your employer may be obliged to verify that your job cannot be filled by a national. Satisfying these conditions can be very difficult in regions of high unemployment.

If you are age twenty-six or younger, a member of the British Commonwealth and traveling in a commonwealth country, you may sometimes obtain a working holiday visa, which allows you to supplement your travel income. Check with embassies for changes regarding the regulations.

American students wishing to work abroad should contact the Work Abroad Department, which sponsors a program enabling you to work in a foreign country for three to six months. The department can be reached at 212 661-1414 extension 1130.

Canadian students should contact Travel CUTS, which offers similar programs and can be reached at 416 977-3703 or by writing 243 College Street, 5th Floor, Toronto, ON, Canada M5T 2Y1.

If you are not a student or member of a commonwealth country, ask for employment information from the visa department of the country you will be visiting.

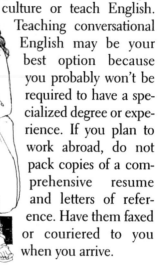

Hospitality, food and beverage industries are typical employers, but don't overlook opportunities to work in agriculture or teach English. Teaching conversational English may be your best option because you probably won't be required to have a specialized degree or experience. If you plan to work abroad, do not pack copies of a comprehensive resume and letters of reference. Have them faxed or couriered to you when you arrive.

IMPORTING

The more adventurous may wish to explore products suitable for an import business back at home. You'll be taking your place in a profession dating back to the dawn of desert and ocean traders, but it's not for the faint of heart.

If in your travels you encounter products that you believe will be of interest back at home, obtain as much information as possible about price, quality, supply and any export conditions. Upon your return home you will need to create a business plan to direct your venture. Any number of books are available to guide the entrepreneur, but you may also want to consider finding a mentor with experience in importing.

TIPS FOR AN IMPORT BUSINESS PLAN

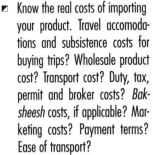

- Know your product. Quality? Durability? Uniqueness?

- Know the real costs of importing your product. Travel accomodations and subsistence costs for buying trips? Wholesale product cost? Transport cost? Duty, tax, permit and broker costs? *Baksheesh* costs, if applicable? Marketing costs? Payment terms? Ease of transport?

- Know your market. Demand? Competition? Retail price?

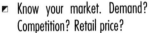

- Know how you will access your market. Distribution channels? Your own shop? Flea markets or craft shows? Wholesale or retail? Door to door?

- Know how you will ship the product home. Land, sea or air? On your person? Will a broker or exporter be required? How much paperwork will be involved? Export packaging?

- Know what problems you might encounter when importing your product. Strikes? Local holidays? Currency fluctuations? Unstable political climates? Coups? Transportation? Money transfers? Consistent, timely supply? Communication? Quality control? Theft in transit?

- Know how you will stay ahead of your competition. Imitation is the sincerest form of flattery, and if you're importing a hot product, expect others to follow in your steps.

In the late 1980s, I operated an import business featuring Peruvian products. Then, almost overnight, the Peruvian economy experienced rampant inflation of 300 per-

cent. *My landed cost for products became more than the market could bear back at home, and I was forced to move the business elsewhere.* – WAYNE

'Juice Man,' Malaysia.

Returning Home

CUSTOMS

However exciting or romantic smuggling may appear, it's not worth the price you'll pay if caught. Customs officers are skilled at spotting smugglers. Any ingenious plan you may devise, they've seen thousands of times before. The best approach is to fill out the declaration card completely and have all items that may need to be inspected readily available. Keep all original receipts and have an itemized list of all purchases.

READJUSTMENT BLUES

The experience of arriving back at home after an extended journey is certain to bring mixed feelings. You welcome the comforts of home and familiar surroundings, but the freedom of overland travel is missing.

On the road you developed routines wholly your own, and you've been responsible to no one but yourself and your traveling companions. The nomad in your soul may have succumbed to the charms of the road, and settling back into your more structured life at home may prove difficult at first. If you yield to a bout of the readjustment blues, remind yourself that freedom is only a state of mind and that home is but another destination in your lifelong travel itinerary. At a practical level, you will readjust faster if you deal quickly with tying up the loose ends of your journey. Check your credit cards for accuracy. Deal with any refunds for unused health or luggage insurance. If you are concerned about residual travel bugs or lingering illness, head to your physician for a checkup. Re-establish contact with your friends, but don't overburden them with tales of your travels.

Finally, give yourself time to shake the jet lag, settle in and savor the experience of coming home. Don't rush back to work unless you absolutely need to. Consider taking a short trip to do some camping or visit some out-of-town friends.

Epilogue

A middle-aged trekker in Nepal, overheard a group of young people ridiculing her for traveling with a Sherpa guide and an entourage of porters carrying everything necessary to her comfort. The young people were self-sufficient, carrying everything they needed on their backs. They left her embarrassed and wondering if their comments were true. Was she robbing herself of the authentic travel experience?

At the end of her trek, she was invited to spend a few days in the village of her guide and porters. Normally, to politely decline their hospitality, she would have excused herself for having to return home soon. But with the young trekkers' comments still stinging, she accepted their offer

Those few days turned into two weeks. During that time she attended a wedding and a funeral. She witnessed a birth, learned how to make and enjoy homemade beer and labored beside the women of the village.

By the time she was ready to leave, she realized that the cultural barrier she had anticipated really didn't exist. Her willingness to experience village life on their terms closed the gap between her well-to-do Chicago lifestyle and the locals' more spartan existence. – WAYNE

Though the traveler's road is sometimes dangerous and not always easy, traveling is a dynamic pursuit with a range of experiences to offer as broad as the Grand Canyon. Budget overland travel is not so much about money as it is about attitude. Shoestring travelers learn resourcefulness and tolerance. They learn patience and acceptance of themselves and the world around them. What they give up in expensive comforts, they gain in authentic experience, which is what travel is really all about. We are in no position to tell you how to take benefit from all you will soon encounter. The information and anecdotes in *The Globetrotter's Guide* are a primer for your adventure; where this book ends, your journey begins. If we could leave you with one thought to ponder as you are about to embark on what is sure to be the trip of your lifetime, it would be what an eager new traveler once told a friend just before leaving: "I know this trip will not be what I expect; I do hope it's all I can't imagine!"

Our sentiments exactly. Have a good time.

Resources

GUIDEBOOKS

Berkeley Guides
Designed more for students on a budget, these guides are geared for the laid-back traveler. They have a jazzy attitude and offer much hard-to-find information on travel for women, gays, lesbians and the disabled.

Birnbaums
A family-oriented series with excellent information on shopping and restaurants, including limited information for travel off-the-beaten track.

Fodor's
This popular series provides information on hotels and restaurants in the moderate to expensive range. It is geared toward business and mainstream travelers.

Frommers
Good guides to low-end and moderately priced hotels and restaurants around the world.

Insight Guides
Full of good photos and informative cultural information, these books are perfect for money-conscious travelers with extra cash to enjoy themselves. The pictures are sure to whet your appetite!

Let's Go
Common with student travelers on a tight budget, the Let's

Go series is geared for those who enjoy having fun. They are particularly good for first-time travelers to Europe.

Lonely Planet
Best-selling guidebooks for budget travelers. They offer detailed maps, practical information and a wealth of description about far-off places. Shoestring Guides are more for the budget traveler and cover a certain geographic region. Travel Survival Kits address all budget levels and are more country specific.

Michelin Guides
Green Guides have artistic, historical and touring information only. Red Guides offer complete ratings of hotels and restaurants for Europe only.

Moon Handbooks
Complete budget guides with abundant cultural, historical and political background information. The series covers areas the world over, including the South Pacific and the United States.

Rough Guides
Rough Guides offer excellent cultural and social information and are targeted toward sophisticated, money-conscious travelers. They also provide more information for women and lesbian travelers than most guides.

Trade and Travel Handbooks
These books are the most detailed and comprehensive travel books available and are targeted to all ranges of travel. Though some people might find the information a little overwhelming, we like having too much rather than not enough. Their best known is the *South American Handbook*, but many more destination guides are now available.

ADVENTURE TRAVEL

Browdy, Dan, ed. *Active Travel Resource Guide.* Hillsdale, NY: Ultimate Ventures, 1995.

Graham, Scott. *Backpacking and Camping in the Developing World.* Berkeley: Wilderness Press, 1988.

Jeffrey, Nan. *Adventuring with Children.* San Francisco: Foghorn Press, 1992.

McMenamin, Paul. *The Ultimate Adventure Sourcebook: A Complete Resource for Adventure and Sports Travel.* Atlanta: Turner Publishing, 1992.

Simmons, James C. *The Big Book of Adventure Travel.* 2nd ed. New York: John Muir, 1995.

CONSCIENTIOUS TRAVEL

Axtell, Roger E. *The Do's and Taboos of Around the World.* 3rd ed. New York: Wiley, 1990.

Axtell, Roger E. *Gestures: The Do's and Taboos of Body Language Around the World.* New York: Wiley, 1991.

Foehr, Stephen. *Eco-Journeys: The World Guide to Ecologically Aware Travel and Adventure.* Chicago: Noble Press, 1992.

Graham, Scott. *Handle With Care: A Guide to Responsible Travel in Developing Countries.* Chicago: Noble Press, 1991.

Grotta, Daniel and Sally W. Grotta. *The Green Travel Sourcebook: A Guide for the Physically Active, the Intellectually Curious, or the Socially Aware.* New York: Wiley, 1992.

Travel for the Disabled and Handicapped

Hecker, Helen. *Travel for the Disabled: A Handbook of Travel Resources and 500 Worldwide Access Guides.* Vancouver, WA: Twin Peaks Press, 1985.

Lewis, Cindy. *A World of Options for the 90's: A Guide to International Educational Exchange, Community Service and Travel for Persons with Disabilities.* Seattle: Mobility International USA, 1990.

Health

Bezruchka, Stephen. *Altitude Illness: Prevention and Treatment.* Seattle: The Mountaineers Books, 1994.

Bezrushka, Stephen. *The Pocket Doctor: Your Ticket to Good Health While Traveling.* 2nd ed. The Mountaineers Books, 1992.

Schroeder, Dirk. *Staying Healthy in Asia, Africa and Latin America.* 4th ed. Emeryville, CA: Moon Publications, 1995.

Speight, Phyllis. *The Traveller's Guide to Homeopathy.* Woodstock: Beekman Publishing, 1990.

Lesbian and Gay Travel

Anderson, Shelley. *Out in the World: International Lesbian Organizing.* Ithaca, NY: Firebrand Books, 1991.

Brandt, Pamela Robin and Lindsay Van Gelder. *Are You Two Together? A Gay and Lesbian Grand Tour of Europe.* New York: Random House, 1991.

MATURE TRAVEL AND TRAVEL WITH CHILDREN

Boga, Stephen. *Camping and Backpacking with Children.* Mechanicsburg, PA: Stackpole Books, 1995.

Butler, Arlene Kay. *Traveling with Children and Enjoying It: A Complete Guide to Family Travel by Car, Plane and Train.* Old Saybrook, CT: Globe Pequot Press, 1991.

Hyman, Mildred. *Elderhostels: The Students' Choice.* 2nd ed. New York: John Muir, 1991.

Malott, Gene and Adele Malott. *Get Up and Go: A Guide for the Mature Traveler.* Oakland, CA: Gateway Books, 1989.

Silverman, Goldie. *Backpacking with Babies and Small Children.* 3rd ed. Berkeley: Wilderness Press, 1986.

Wheeler, Maureen. *Travel with Children.* Oakland, CA: Lonely Planet, 1995.

Williams, Anita and Merrimac Dillon. *The Fifty-Plus Traveler's Guidebook: Where to Go, Where to Stay, What to Do.* New York: St. Martin's Press, 1991.

STUDENT AND VOLUNTEER TRAVEL

Gilpin, Robert and Caroline Fitzgibbons. *Time Out: Taking a Break from School to Travel, Work and Study in the U.S. and Abroad.* New York: Simon and Schuster, 1992.

McMillon, Bill. *Volunteer Vacations: Short Term Adventures That Will Benefit You and Others.* 5th rev. ed. Chicago: Chicago Review Press, 1991.

Ocko, Stephanie. *Environmental Vacations: Volunteer Projects to Save the Planet.* 2nd ed. New York: John Muir Publications, 1992.

Sewell, Hilary. *Working Holidays.* London, UK: Central Bureau for Educational Visits and Exchanges, 1982.

WOMEN'S TRAVEL

Bond, Marybeth, ed. *Travelers' Tales: A Woman's Word.* Sebastopol, CA: Travelers' Tales, c/o O'Reilley and Associates, 1995.

Davies, Miranda and Natania Jansz. *Women Travel: Adventures, Advice and Experience.* New York: Penguin, 1990.

Davies, Miranda and Laura Longrigg. *Half the Earth: Women's Experiences of Travel Worldwide.* New York: Penguin, 1986.

Hubbard and Wass. *Outdoor Woman: A Handbook to Adventure.* Mastermedia, 1992.

Jansz, Natania, ed. *More Women Travel: Adventures and Advice from More than 60 Countries.* 2nd ed. New York: Penguin, 1995.

Jayawardena, Kumari. *Feminism and Nationalism in the Third World.* Atlantic Highlands, NJ: Humanities Press, 1986.

Morgan, Robin, ed. *Sisterhood Is Global: The First Anthology of Writings from the International Women's Movement.* New York: Doubleday, 1984.

New Internationalist Publication Staff. *Women: A World Report.* New York: Oxford University Press, 1987.

Zepatos, Thalia. *A Journey of One's Own: Uncommon Advice for the Independent Women Traveler.* Portland: Eighth Mountain Press, 1992.

WORKING OVERSEAS

Griffith, Susan. *Work Your Way Around the World.* 7th ed. Princeton: Peterson's Guides, 1995.

Central Bureau for Educational Visit and Exchanges Staff. *Working Holidays: The Complete Guide to Seasonal Jobs.* 4th ed. Cincinnati: Seven Hills Books, 1995.

INTERNET RESOURCES

Travel services and information continue to proliferate on the World Wide Web. Following are some we've found useful.

Books and Guides

Fodor's
http://www.fodors.com

Interactive Travel Guides
http://www.travelpage.com/

Lonely Planet
http://www.lonelyplanet.com.au/lp.htm

Rough Guides
http://www.hotwired.com/rough/

Recreation Travel Library
http://www.travel-library.com/

Rec. Travel Library
ftp://ftp.cc.umanitoba.ca/rec-travel/README.html

The Travel Bug Bookstore
http://www.swifty.com/tbug/

Ulysses Travel Guides
http://www.ulysses.ca/

World Travel Guide
http://www.wtgonline.com/

Tickets and Fares

Encounter Overland
http://www.encounter.co.uk

E-Travel Website
http://www.e-travel.com

EUnet Traveller
http://traveller.eu.net/

Global Network Navigator: GNN
http://nearnet.gnn.com/mata/travel/index.html

Green Tortoise Adventure Travel
http://www.greentortoise.com

Internet Travel Network
http://www.itn.net/cgi/getitn/index/

Preview Travel
http://www.previewtravel.com/index.html

Surrogate Travel and Mosaic
http://nemo.ncsl.nist.gov/~sressler/projects/nav/surr/nav-
Surr.html

Ticket Planet: Lowest Priced International Airfares
http://www.ticketplanet.com/

The Travel Connection
http://ctd.com/travel/travel.html

Travel Corner
http://www.travelcorner.com/

Travel Cuts
http://www.travelcuts.com/

TravLtips: Cruise and Freighter Travel Association
http://www.travltips.com/

Web Travel Index
http://www.traveler.net/two/

General Information

Berlitz Language Courses
http://www.berlitz.com/

Centers for Disease Control
http://www.cdc.gov/travel/travel.html

Center for Disease Control and Prevention
http://www.cdc.gov/

City.Net
http://www.city.net/

The Electronic Embassy
http://www.embassy.org/

The Embassy Page
http://www.finnemb.nw.dc.us/web/gsis/embpage.html

EUnet Traveller
http://traveller.eu.net:80/

Foreign Languages for Travelers
http://www.travlang.com/languages/

Fun Travel Info
http://www.mit.edu:8001/afs/athena.mit.edu/user/p/j
/pjb/www/travel.html

Hostels Around the World
http://www.hostels.com

Local Times Around the World
http://www.hilink.com.au/times/

Mapquest: Maps and Atlases
http://www.mapquest.com/

National Holidays
http://www.sas.upenn.edu/African_Studies/Country_Speci
fic/Holidays.html

Ten-10
http://www.ten-io.com

Tips for Travellers
http://www.webfoot.com/travel/tips/tips.top.html

Travel Forums
http://www.explore.com/Explorer_forums.html

Travel Health Information
http://www.intmed.mcw.edu/travel.html

The Travel Lane
http://www.mit.edu:8001/people/kebooth/welcome.html

Traveller Information Services Master Index
http://www.traveller.com/

Traveler's Checklist
http://www.ag.com/Travelers/Checklist/safety

Travel Related Phone Numbers
http://www.mit.edu:8001/people/wchuang/travel/travel

Travel World Insurance
http://www.omnitravel.com/007insurance.html

Universal Currency Converter
http://www.xe.net/currency.htm

VISA ATM Locations Worldwide
http://www.visa.com/visa/locator/atm_region.html

U.S. State Department Travel Warnings and Info Sheets
http://www.stolaf.edu/network/travel-advisories.html/

Visa, Passport and Entry Requirements
http://gnn.com/gnn/meta/travel/res/visa.html

Women Traveler
http://www.libertynet.org/anthec/

Yahoo Travel Links
http://www.yahoo.com/Recreation/Travel

Airlines

Aeroflot
http://www.aeroflot.org/

Air New Zealand
http://www.iconz.co.nz/airnz/airnz.html

British Airways
http://www.british-airways.com/

Canadian Airlines
http://www.cdnair.ca/

Lufthansa
gopher://gopher.enews.com:2100/11/travel/lufthansa/

Northwest Airlines
http://www.nwa.com/

Quantas Airways Limited
http://www.quantas.com/

Royal Dutch Airlines
http://www.klm.nl/

Singapore Airlines
http://www.singaporeair.com/

Thai Airways International
http://www.thaiair.com/

Trans World Airlines
http://www.twa.com/

United Airlines
http://www.ual.com/home/

NOTES

Notes

NOTES

ABOUT THE AUTHORS

Wayne Smits

A short story writer and self-confessed wanderer, Wayne has always had a keen interest in that which lay beyond the mere mechanics of overland travel. His love for the road developed at an early age, and since then he has rallied those interests into a filing cabinet of practical experiences and a successful seven year stint as an importer. When not traveling or writing, he lectures for groups like the International Youth Hostel Association on the subject of travel safety and security.

Caryl E. Dolinko

Having traveled on her own to over sixty countries, Caryl E. Dolinko teaches travel courses for the Vancouver School Board and is a frequent radio talk show guest. She is an avid photographer with work on display in numerous cafés and galleries. Caryl studied anthropology and sociology at Simon Fraser University. She continues to travel for pleasure and with the hope of achieving a better understanding of the world and its people.